ARTICLES

VOLUME 1

TOM FEXAS

2018

Copyright © by Regina Fexas

All rights reserved.

No part of this book may be reproduced in any form or by any electronic or mechanical means, including information storage and retrieval systems, without written permission from the editor, except for the use of brief quotations in a book review.

Independently Published

Printed in the USA

ISBN: 9781717917195

"I first met Tom in the early 80's, after seeing one of his designs out in the Bahama's in the late 70's. I was captivated with the styling, and even more impressed with the performance and efficiency. Little did I know that this meeting would lead to a long and wonderful lifetime friendship. There were occasions where Tom and I would talk daily for long stretches about designs and ideas, and he challenged the norm every time he could, always to make things better. Tom was an extraordinary naval architect who was dedicated to the "Art" of the design, its flow, its efficiency, and how it moved through the water. Every nuance, every detail, was of the utmost importance, and the results showed in performance and the way each boat looked. Tom used to say the size of a well designed boat that had the proper proportions was difficult to know from a distance, and that was certainly true of each one of his. He was a man of his word, his handshake mattered, and he carried himself with respect and honor.
...His Legacy will carry on well past the physical presence of his designs..."

Dick Peterson – President of Mikelson Yachts

Contents

1985

FEBRUARY - Sailing is Silly

MARCH - Yacht Fakery!

APRIL - Yacht Styling: The Squares vs. the Rounds

MAY - A "Revolutionary" Sportsfishing Boat

JUNE - Off My Chest

JULY - Confessions

AUGUST - Confessions, Part 2

SEPTEMBER - Bring Back the Commuter

OCTOBER - Triple Screws for the Masses

NOVEMBER - The Fourth Greatest Lie

DECEMBER - Transom Pollution

1986

JANUARY - Mortadella Memories

FEBRUARY - Impressions of the Hamburg Boat Show

MARCH - In a Slump

APRIL - *Transom Sewage*
MAY - *Magical Miami*
JUNE - *Good Morning Hong Kong*
JULY - *Where Have all the Steelcraft Gone?*
AUGUST - *"Sportsfishing" Brazilian Style*
SEPTEMBER - *The Green Icon*
OCTOBER - *Things I Hate*
NOVEMBER - *Pioneers of American Power Yachting*
DECEMBER - *A Plea for Low Tech - December*

1987

JANUARY - *Where the Boats Are*
FEBRUARY - *The Blobs are Coming!*
MARCH - *Don't Put Down the New York Boat Show*

Sailing is Silly (or, sooner or later one must face the fact that a so-called "Sailboat" is merely a Power Boat with a funny cabin and masts)

As a designer of power vessels for many years, I have dealt with many types of people. They all have different ideas concerning their ultimate boat but there is a common thread in their thinking: they believe that a proper boat is one which has sturdy engines thrumming beneath their feet. Engines that can be relied upon to get them out of tough situations and deliver their yachts to their destination at a pre-determined time. But every once in a while, strange types of yachtsmen are encountered. They seem to revel in rope burns and salt water running down their necks. They speak in a strange language using words like "clew" and "weather helm". They speak ill of us powerboaters and oftentimes wear bright green pants (with little flags on them) and funny hats. They usually stand at an angle somewhat off perpendicular. These fellows are called "sailors" and it is to this select group of yachtsmen that I have this to say: C'MON GUYS, COME CLEAN AND ADMIT IT! SAILING IS A RATHER SILLY EXERCISE AND MOST SAILBOATS ARE REALLY ONLY POWERBOATS WITH FUNNY LOOKING CABINS AND MASTS! (That should get their attention.) After this blasphemy, I will document with facts why this is so.

At first glance, the concept is intriguing – a vessel that moves across the sea powered by beautiful, quiet, clean, (and importantly) free air. Sounds good! No fuel expense, no fumes, no noise, no pollution. Sounds *real* good! But wait! There are some drawbacks. See, the boat doesn't directly move when the wind blows. No, you must first hang funny shaped pieces of cloth on tall sticks. Because these sticks are so tall, they must be supported by a complicated web of wires. The pieces of cloth must be controlled through a system of pulleys by a maze of strings attached to them. Sounds complicated, doesn't it?

But wait! There's more. Because of these cloths strung up so high on the sticks, the vessel must be balanced by a heavy mass of weight placed down low in the hull. Because the hull will slide sideways when the wind pushes on the cloths, a strange, big, flat appendage must be fitted below the hull greatly increasing draft and restricting areas the boat may be cruised in. Sometimes, the heavy weight is attached to the appendage, thereby creating a great strain on the hull. The deep hull form resulting requires that the inhabitants of this vessel must live, eat, and sleep in a dark, narrow cave in the water that is much wider on top than it is on the bottom.

There's still more! This cave in the water tilts at varying angles when underway: sometimes to the left, sometimes to the right. The inhabitants must learn to dwell on the low side of the cave, wedged into corners or hung by straps. Food must be served on a table that swivels and getting around is easier if one leg is longer than the other. Because the cave floats so low, water is constantly finding its way down into it. Little holes cut in the sides of the cave admit small shafts of light. Once on deck, things aren't so simple either for it is nearly impossible to walk from stern to bow without choking yourself on one of the strings or wires. Additionally, there are funny contraptions placed in your path on deck which will trip you, and toss you overboard.

Well, that's about it – except for one more little drawback: due to the whimsical wind, you never know when (or _if_) you will reach your destination, and more importantly, YOU CAN'T POINT THE DAMN BOAT IN THE DIRECTION YOU WOULD LIKE TO TRAVEL!

Some contend that a sailboat is non-polluting and silent. I guess this is so, but consider: a big stick violently swinging in the breeze from side to side just above your head might be considered the ultimate in airborne pollution when it smacks you on the cranium. Silent? Ever hear those wires and strings slapping against those sticks in an otherwise quiet harbor?

But sailing is fun, isn't it? Well, if one is to perform this action called "sailing", one must rise early from his cave for there is much to do before one can actually "sail". Big bags must be dragged out on deck and the large cloths must be pulled out of them to be strung up on the sticks. This is only accomplished by a great amount of cranking, pulling, and general scurrying about the decks. After a day of "sailing", the now wet cloths must be taken off the sticks, stuffed in the bags, and dragged back down into the cave.

But what about the benefits? Well, there's good news and bad news. The good news is that, yes, if you're willing to put up with the above mentioned complications, you can, indeed, move across the water for free – except if there's no wind. The bad news is that to alleviate this little problem, a unique solution was arrived at. INSTALL AN ENGINE. An engine? Yes, friends, when things get hairy or when anchoring, or when there's no wind, or during docking/undocking, the engine is simply switched on. What a great idea! Which seems to bring us back to square one. If engines are to be installed anyhow, why go through the expense of all those cloths, sticks, wires, strings, cranks, and pulleys? And doesn't this piece of machinery below decks render a "sailboat" simply a power boat with funny-looking cabins and masts? C'mon guys, trade in those bright green pants (with little flags on them) for a pair of greasy coveralls and admit it. SAILING IS SILLY! Case closed.

February 1985

Yacht Fakery!

The great American art of making one's boat appear to be something other than it is

I am told it started in the late 50's at Capri Marina in Port Washington, New York, a town well known for its "keeping up with the Joneses" image. Back then, Chris Craft Constellations were lined up row upon row, at the few marinas that existed at the time -- sort of like Hatterases are today.

Seems one of these "Connie" owners decided he needed (or wanted) radar. One day, a radar dome appeared on his cabin top. Now, one wouldn't think that a simple act such as this would start a nationwide trend, but it did. Needless to say, the following weekend the strange dome made his neighbors a bit uneasy and envious. Pretty soon, domes started sprouting up on cabin tops throughout the marina. Constellation owners in the neighboring Riviera Marina picked up on the trend and soon it was spreading across the United States. Radar domes almost became mandatory on vessels over 40'. This would have normally made radar manufacturers happy except for one thing: HALF THE DOMES

WERE DUMMIES CONTAINING NO ANTENNA OR GUTS! That's right, empty radar enclosures erected solely for the purpose of impressing (or keeping up with) one's marina neighbors and the start of a great trend in modern yachting. Yes, yacht fakery, the great American art of making one's boat appear to be something other than it actually is – was underway.

Next, we saw davits installed that never hoisted a tender, dummy flying bridge enclosures sans controls and seats and anchors nestled in salty-looking hawse pipes on vessels that never left the dock. There were rumors that at Marina Del Rey, in California, there were new yachts at the marina delivered WITHOUT ENGINES having cases of wine in the engine compartments acting as ballast.

Soon we were seeing fully festooned large fishing machines sporting 40' stayed outriggers, erector set double deck tuna towers, $10,000 chrome fishing chairs, transom doors, gin poles, an array of $2,000 fishing rods, bait prep centers and anything else that might impress one's neighbor. Problem was that these machines NEVER TROLLED FOR ANYTHING OTHER THAN BIKINI-CLAD MAIDENS ON THE DOCKS! The outriggers and gewgaws were, of course, bait.

Then came the era of heavy, stout cruisers that appeared as little ships -- fully capable of crossing large bodies of water -- even oceans -- at the drop of a flopper stopper. They cruised at 7 or 8 knots with strong, slow turning diesel power. Most had massive anchor pulpits and anchoring gear and small, square windows that would resist the great seas that could come crashing aboard. Some even had smoke stacks to complete the effect! These vessels were called "trawler yachts" and most were used for trans-intercoastal waterway voyages from restaurant to restaurant. A waste to be sure, but one really did look and feel like John Wayne when on the bridge of one of these little ships. And they <u>certainly</u> served the purpose of thoroughly intimidating your marina neighbor in his lightly built cabin cruiser.

   The next development in this trend has been proposed by a friend and business associate. Being in the boating business, his finger is on the pulse of the American boating community. His idea concerns the currently popular breed of macho boats – the long, skinny, deep V'd, high powered ocean racing runabouts so commonly seen in our waterways. His scheme is simple but brilliant. These boats are very expensive due to their complicated, high powered multiple engines and elaborate drive systems. Yet, most of these craft are boulevard (canal) cruisers never venturing out to sea or exceeding the "no wake" speed of seven knots. It turns out that these vessels are even more powerful bait than the sportsfishermen! A guy can start his trek up the waterway alone but will soon be surrounded by a bevy of scantily clad women oohing and aahing over the boat and, hopefully, its pilot.

   Well, the thinking goes like this: since 95% of these "ocean racers" never leave their local canals or harbors, why not put the buyer's money where it most counts -- on image rather than substance. His idea is simply to create the meanest, most sinister, evil looking craft for the least money. Consequently, the hull would be painted flat black all over --

bottom, topsides, deck, and cockpit. A barbed ram would be affixed to the bow (sort of like the one on the "Nautilus" in Jules Verne 20,000 Leagues Under The Sea). A gaping shark's mouth with huge teeth would be painted on the bow with blood dripping from one corner and entrails dangling out the other. WE'RE TALKING MEAN HERE! All deck hardware would be forged of wrought iron and the cockpit upholstery would be of stiff, scratchy rhinoceros hide. The steering wheel would be replaced with studded reins. Yes, all in all, a totally dominating canal racer.

But, here is where the real genius comes in. Since these boats are restricted by the "no wake" zones and can't exceed 7 knots anyhow, why have two or three massive, complicated, and expensive engines/drivelines at all? Why not install a single 30 h.p. engine, such as a Universal Atomic Four, a totally reliable, cheap engine that's done yeoman's duty in the bilges of sailboats for years!

The engine would be connected to a simple ¾" bronze shaft turning a sailboat prop. There it is! A cheap, simple, easy to maintain power plant capable of driving a vessel at the maximum legal speed of 7 knots. A truly practical arrangement – except for one thing: THE SOUND. Part of the attraction of these vessels is the noise they make. They simply wouldn't be the same without a brapping, unmuffled exhaust. Now for the coup de grace. The Atomic Four's anemic 1-1/2" exhaust manifold is connected to four 8" wrought iron megaphone headers leading out the transom! A water pump belted off the engine would move massive amounts of water out the pipes. A high powered, 150 watt per channel stereo tape system would be installed with speakers hidden in the transom. When the engine is started, a cassette tape of, say, rail fuel dragsters at the Winternational Drag Races would automatically activate and blare out the transom completing the image. Yes, a true breakthrough in putting money where it _really_ counts. Imagine! Cruising up the waterway in your sailboat engine powered, deep-V racer with deafening exhaust sounds of a nitro burning, V-8 Hemi Chrysler emanating from your exhausts, penetrating to the marrow with every exhaust pulse.

Once in a lifetime (if you're lucky) you might hit upon a sure fired idea that you _know_ will make you a man of true wealth and enable you to retire at a young age to the South Seas. Well, I'm packing my bags for Tahiti because I've come up with marine fakery to end all marine fakery and carry the trend to its logical and ultimate conclusion. I live in Florida, see, where people just _love_ waterfront homes. But what's a waterfront home without a dock and a big, expensive yacht behind it, right? Trouble is that while people would love to have a yacht behind their house, most do not because boats are expensive to buy and always seem to need some paint or varnish or an expensive piece of gear that has fallen off or broken. Then there's those troublesome docklines which can trip you while you're strolling on your dock. WELL... HERE IT IS, WORLD, the ultimate fakery -- BILLBOARD YACHTS! My idea is this: flat pieces of plywood would be fitted together edge-to-edge and cut to the silhouette of any yacht desired and painted on both sides to suit. This will enable you to have absolutely any yacht you desire. The Queen of England's "Britannia"? No problem. Perhaps a three-point hydroplane or that 72' sportsfisherman you've always wanted. The billboard yacht can simply be nailed to your dock so that from the house or to the envious eyes of passers-by on the water, it would appear that you have a big, expensive yacht behind your house. Yes, the money should be rolling in any day now.

In the meantime, look over to the boat in the next slip -- you know, the one with the luscious half-dressed blonde that always distracts you. Now...look closely..."ARE YOU SURE SHE'S REAL"

March 1985

Yacht Styling: the Squares vs the Rounds

I can't believe it's finally happened. Italian yacht stylists have finally rediscovered CURVES! Let's face it, the Italians usually call the shots insofar as design trends are concerned whether it be in yachts, automobiles or furniture. After years of designing yachts, most of which looked like Pablo Picasso had taken up yacht design (with superstructures looking like they were formed of folded cardboard), smooth, rounded, sensuous forms are just starting to appear in some of their latest boats and I predict, within a year, this trend will be widespread.

As a lone advocate for rounded, organic boat styling these past years, it seemed to me that since the mid-60's, boats have looked like they were planned by designers who possessed only straightedges and didn't know about French curves, splines, or circle templates. The Italian boats, for the most part, were startling but never what one would call beautiful -- most of them looking like "Battle Star Galactica" sitting atop an ocean racing hull. There were funny bumps, creases, wows, hiccups, indentations, protuberances and windows going off at different, crazy angles with no relationship to one another. There were structures that, as an engineer, I can only describe as "funny things" sticking up out of the superstructure at different angles for no apparent reason. Looking at some of these boats kind of made me itch. A few bucked the trend -- Riva is one that comes to mind -- but mostly, it was "Kirk to Enterprise" time for the Italians. American boats were not as radical, but were still, basically, straight and square.

You don't fool with Mother Nature. Consider if an egg were to be cube-shaped. Not only would it be structurally fragile, but it would be pure hell for a hen to lay and thereafter incubate...OUCH! Why aren't there square tree trunks? Why aren't water droplets cube-shaped? And why don't ducks have chines and flat bottoms? The answer is that nature has forsaken hard corners for rounded forms that are more structurally sound, more aero or hydrodynamic, or simply more beautiful. It's funny, the Italians are known for their love and appreciation of beautiful women. You'd think they would have caught on sooner. Picasso may have drawn women with cube-shaped breasts and sharp corners on their legs and buttocks but you could never imagine a real woman like that... could you? (As a matter of fact, I DID know a woman like that once...but that's another story.) No... beautiful women do not come with square corners and the lusty Italians, more than anyone, should know this.

From the days of the early power boats, marine shapes have mimicked the automotive shapes of the day. The term "auto boats" became popular in the 20's and 30's for this reason. Of course, everything runs in circles. And, just as ladies' hemlines go up and down, stylists continually vacillate between roundness and sharp corners. Following the auto industry, sharp, angular superstructures of the 20's gave way to rounded, billowy forms in the 30's and continued after the war. In the 50's things got extreme with some cars looking like big, melted marshmallows (remember the '50 Mercury and the '50 Dodge?). In the mid-60's we started seeing sharply creased automobiles replacing the round ones and in the 70's the trend continued – razor – edged, wedge-shaped automobiles were the rage. Yes, there were some dissenters that rebelled either on artistic principles or of economic necessity (which required them to utilize tooling from the round eras). Jaguar is a good example. Jaguar has always been round and they never seem to go out of style. Their beautiful XJ6 sedan designed in the early 60's is still an eye-catcher today. For a good example of automotive design trends, let's follow the Corvette from its inception in 1953 to today. Conceived in the early 50's, the first body style was very round looking somewhat like a puffy cloud. This basic style was carried from 1953 to 1962. The '63, first of the "mid-year" Corvettes, marked a transition between roundness and razor-edge. Mid-year 'Vettes were produced from '63 through '67. The '68 Corvette was something entirely different. It employed sharp ridges, creases, and hard angles all over its body. This body style ran from '68 to '82. In 1983 we saw the all-new Corvette introduced and, lo' and behold, it was round again! The boating industry seems to lag the automobile industry, as far as styling goes, by about five years. In the 50's Chris Crafts were, perhaps, some of the roundest boats ever produced, with bulbous stems, rounded sheer lines, rounded cabin tops, and rounded edges everywhere on the cabin. Remember, these were <u>wooden</u> production boats so the workmanship on these boats was something to be admired. The first Hatteras (that's the famous 41' sportfisherman) was of rounded styling in the early '60's. By the mid-60's, boat superstructures began to square up and this theme has been carried on to this day for over <u>twenty years</u> with few exceptions.

But now, all is changing! Sensuous curves are appearing and this important trend cannot be overlooked. At my urging, Cheoy Lee took the plunge in 1980. Trojan's new "meter" boats are round and the trend is expanding in the U.S. In Italy, Tullio Abbate has just come out with a 45' Magnum-type speedboat called "Exception". Instead of a hard corner where the deck meets the sheer, a heavy radius exists similar to the beautiful mahogany Greavette streamlined speedboats from the '30's. The "Exception's" transom curves in two planes -- athwart ships and down towards the water. In all, curves are a very refreshing change -- and one that is sure to be imitated by other boat builders.

I have come up with a fool-proof way to determine if an object is of good design. It is simply: does it feel good to clean it? Yes... Does it feel good to clean it? I had a 1980 sharp edged Corvette for years that never gave me any pleasure when I washed it. When a new Isuzu Impulse came into my life I found I enjoyed the hell out of washing that car with its beautiful, rounded contours. The same applies to kitchen objects... and boats. Corners, it seems, are as unfriendly to hands or brushes or sponges as they are to water or air.

If I know the Italians, they will carry their newly discovered roundness to the extreme and, soon, their boats will look like Crayolas left out in the sun too long or, perhaps, a well-used candle. After this happens, you can rest assured that sharp creased will be back again. We should all celebrate the rediscovery of curves in yacht design and enjoy it while it lasts. Now... about that woman with the cubes...

April 1985

A "Revolutionary" Sportsfishing

Two months ago I wrote an article in which my great idea concerning billboard yachts was introduced. I must admit that I did think this idea would make me a very wealthy man, however, the proceeds have not yet started rolling in and I am beginning to wonder if they ever will. I have therefore decided to come clean and introduce an idea that I have held under lock and key for many many years. This one puts the billboard yachts idea to shame and is so good that I just know that its time has come and that I am going to make it BIG. I'm talking millions big here. Gucci leather underwear big, Forbes 400 big and Phil Donahue show big. This probably will be the last article I write, since handling my portfolio will be a full time job.

The other day we were sitting around the ol' design office discussing a subject that has been bandied about worldwide for maybe fifty years. The best yacht designers and experts in the field have debated this subject for all this time and, yet, still have not come up with an acceptable solution. The problem is: WHAT EXACTLY IS THE IDEAL SPORTS FISHING BOAT? We're not talking about a floating Fountain Bleu with a cockpit attached, but a "blood and guts" type fishing boat for the guy who takes his fishing seriously and cares little about other amenities. I have, over the past sixteen years, designed scores of sports fishing boats, each a little different than the other to suit the whims and fancies of their owners. If one wants something on the left, the other will certainly want it on the right and another will want it in the middle! Then there's always someone who wants it off- center! Logic can seldom be employed in fishing boat decisions because everything is so subjective. Well, the boat I am proposing here is so logical that nobody will be able to dispute the idea. As you may or may not know (or care) two age old fishing problems are the relationship of the fishing chair to the cockpit envelope and the maneuverability of the vessel itself. When a fish is hooked, action gets wild in the cockpit. If the boat is too wide, the fishing line can snag on the corners of the transom and the fish (which, by the way, is <u>always</u> a record fish) will be lost. Even the best of today's fishing boats lack the instantaneous maneuverability required for backing down on a fish that erratically changes its direction of flight many times during battle. There have been many attempts to solve these two problems -- some fishing boats have been designed with rounded cockpit corners to eliminate line snagging, other boats have been built super light with huge power plants to wrench the boat around in different directions as necessary. These are, however only partial solutions.

Well true fisherman, I am proud to say your problems are <u>over</u>. I am happy to introduce the new line of DOUGHNUT

SPORTS FISHING BOATS! Yes, you read it right, doughnuts as in round with a hole in the middle! Think of it! A boat 12' in diameter with an outboard motor set into a well in its center and a fighting chair set directly over it. The chair is free to pivot in any direction and, since the hull is never more than 6' from the center of the chair in any direction, the line will always clear the hull side. Not just at the stern but <u>all</u> <u>around</u> the entire vessel. By rotating the outboard motor and applying power, instant maneuverability in any direction is available.

Actually, this idea has been "around" (sorry about that) for a number of years, but applied to the wrong type of boat. Round life boats are commonplace and, in the '50's OMC introduced a showboat which was round and powered by two outboards. This is an excellent example of an idea that was very close to the mark but just missed for one reason or another -- like the guy who wrote the song "Tea For Three" that never went anywhere and was really upset when someone wrote a song called "Tea For Two" that was a smash hit. In the case of the OMC round boat, it was the same type of thing. They were introducing the boat as a <u>runabout</u>. If only the boat had been introduced as a sports fisherman, who knows what the consequences would have been. It's my guess that today round Hatteras and Bertram sports fishing boats would be commonplace had OMC hit the mark in the '50's.

There are many supplemental benefits to the doughnut boat. People who forget where bow, stern, port and starboard is need worry no more -- there IS no bow, stern, port or starboard. The bow may be anywhere you assign it and, in fact, the bow and stern can be one in the same! Docking will be much simplified eliminating the hassle of bringing the bow to the dock, then swinging the stern in. One would simply roll into the dock bouncing from pile to pile. No problem! Anchoring, too, would be much simplified as the anchor may be thrown from any quadrant of the vessel.

I can see it all now. Fleets of Doughnut Sports fishing boats, fully rigged with flying bridges, tuna towers, stayed outriggers and rocket launchers competing head to head, doughnut to doughnut in tournaments around the world. It boggles the mind. Even now, I can hear the scratch of pens in checkbooks. I think I'd better put out a bigger mailbox to handle the volume...

May 1985

Off My Chest

Sometimes, you just have to do it... Come out and say what you think about all the little things that are bugging you. Well, this is one of those times -- so please bear with me.

Revenge of the Ragbaggers

Lord, now I've done it -- the raghangers are after me! Ever since my article entitled "Sailing is Silly" was published, I have received many irate letters and have been the subject of unfavorable articles in sailing oriented publications. After all this abuse, I realized I left out a very important ragbagger characteristic: MANY OF THEM HAVE ABSOLUTELY NO SENSE OF HUMOR. There was some cupcake who wrote from California -- the land of fruits and nuts -- stating in his letter he was so upset with the article he didn't know whether to "---- or go blind". This guy was a live aboard on a Maine built gaff rigged sailboat. I can just see this poor bearded soul clearing a spot in the rubble of his cabin to take pen in hand and respond to the terrible things I said in the article. Another humorless scribe writing for a small paper in Annapolis was so upset he saw fit to devote a whole page in response to my story. Only the good Reverend Norris was intelligent enough to respond to humor and satire with the same. Since I have obviously hit a nerve here, and never being one to shy away from battle, I'll throw a few more dynamite sticks into the fire: When was the last time you heard of anybody switching from a powerboat to a sailboat? People go from sail to power all the time (oftentimes when they have reached retirement age and have attained a modicum of common sense. Why are sailboat sales so lousy these days? And what about the new high powered high speed "sailboats" that are on the market -- the ones that you can do 20 knots under power? Yes, keep those cards and letters coming in you poor, humorless, misguided souls. And don't look back... a power boat may be gaining on you!

Outlaws

Since I am in a fighting mood, I would like to salute the Florida Marine Patrol for their absolute inability to grasp the obvious. Four Midnight Laces -- three 52's and one 44 footer were cruising south in the channel west of Marathon, Florida Keys, on a bright sunny afternoon following one another in "line ahead" formation doing our best to dodge the crab pots in this area that are strewn about like shredded styrofoam. Granted, Midnight Laces are black and possess a rather sinister beauty but, come on guys, THIS WAS RIDICULOUS! Running at about 20 knots and minding our business, the last boat noticed a marine patrol "squad boat" overtaking them. Thinking nothing of it we proceeded. The "squad boat" overtook us and "pulled over" the lead boat. Of course, we all stopped and stood by to see what the problem was. Low and behold, on the horizon appeared THREE more marine patrol boats converging on our position (lest the other three Midnight Laces scatter). It seemed some jerk seeing the four black boats running together thought we "looked suspicious" and dutifully reported us to the marine patrol. This is bad enough, but you'd think when the marine patrol overtook us and saw that we were four cruising boats he would have given us a polite wave as he passed by. But no, he boarded the lead boat and engaged in about ten minutes of silly conversation before departing, satisfied but probably very disappointed at not having cracked one of the biggest drug rings in South Florida. Did they think people who wanted to run illegal substances would actually choose FOUR Midnight Laces -- probably the most "high profile" vessels afloat? And would they be running in shimmering sunny daylight together? As it turned out, the lead boat while idling during the encounter picked up a crab pot on her port screw and subsequently damaged one engine. COME ON GUYS, A LITTLE COMMON SENSE HERE!

Boat Show Bags

And while I'm at it, I have another beef. You know the plastic bags they hand out at boat shows for collecting catalogs and brochures? The problem is THE DAMN

HANDLES ALWAYS BREAK and you end up with your carefully selected catalogs strewn all over the floor. This usually happens in some wonderful place like the bathroom or near the refreshment stands -- the ones with mustard and soda all over the floor. Needless to say recovering your brochures from a wet or mustard covered floor isn't much fun and, besides, the brochures are sticky and smell funny afterwards. This year in Miami, I picked up a bag with a name like "Milties Electronics" on it. Of course, the handle promptly broke after one or two sheets were inserted into it but this was to be expected from a bag with a wimpy name like "Milties Electronics". So, I undertook a search for a bag that would hold. I passed up more silly bags with names like "Cuddle Boat" and "Naval Lint Cove -- A Retirement Development". No, I was looking for a REAL bag. After a long search and much disappointment, I came up with a black bag that had emblazoned on it in white "ZF – ZAHNRADFABRIK FRIEDRICHSHAFEN"! I use their excellent transmissions all the time! Here was a REAL bag. A bag that could take it. A bag with German engineering. I took four. Wouldn't you know it, on my way out of the show while walking to the parking lot with all bags brimming to the seams with hundreds of catalogs carefully selected over a span of five days, the bags let go. It happened when I was steeping over an exhibitor who was "resting" in the gutter covering him with information about innovative new products like pitch less props (for boats that never leave the dock), women's spike heeled boat shoes and water makers that make saltwater from fresh (for bluewater sailors landlocked in freshwater lakes). Well, what could I do? The "resting exhibitor" distributed the papers and catalogs over his body to act as a shield from the cool night air, and went back to sleep. I didn't have the heart to wake him. I do hope he enjoys the information on the new inflatable boat bars (for boats without room for permanent bars) complete with inflating stools and footrests.

Boat Show Babes

Talking about boat shows, I noticed a great lack of feminine pulchritude at the last Miami Boat Show. Usually, beautiful women provide great competition for the boats at the show. More than one man has been nearly decapitated walking into an overhanging transom platform (or nearly lost the reason for looking at women at all by walking into a pointy bowed outboard boat whose prow was at a strategic height) while his eyes were on some "lovely" in short shorts and a see-through top (or a short top with see-through shorts). As usual, I have some theories which are in no particular order:

1. Women in boating are getting older, outgrowing short shorts and see through tops and graduating to log shorts and bulky jackets in order to hide rather than reveal.

2. The boats and exhibits are becoming more spectacular than the women.

3. The really spectacular women hang around the Miami Grand Prix because they realize they don't have to put up with boats and their strange owners.

Of course, there were exceptions but, generally, it was a disappointing boat show despite the terrific boats and record sales.

Gee, I feel better now!

June 1985

Confessions

This is not a pretty story. It is one of addiction, cure and relapse. Those of you with weak stomachs might want to turn the pages. This story is the REAL THING! Coming out of the closet and admitting an aberration is never easy, but I present my story in the hope that it may help other people with similar problems. My addiction had been dormant for five years. I really thought I was cured until an incident that occurred last week...

I was introduced to boating at the age of five months in the spring of 1941 aboard my Dad's nearly new 32' Wheeler (I would have started sooner, but "Antonia", as she was called, was not commissioned until springtime!). From that time, until five years ago, I was a constant boat owner, either through my family or, later, on my own. Getting rid of my last boat five years ago was, I thought, a smart move. I was really too busy to enjoy boating and the boat I owned required much upkeep, which I had no time for. The once magnificent vessel was slowly turning to Silly Putty before my eyes in the damp, warm South Florida climate. I thought I could fulfill my boating needs by playing with some of the boats I designed and, over the past five years, the dock behind my house has secured a number of them including a 48' Cheoy Lee Sportsfisherman and a 52' Midnight Lace. These boats, however, were only on loan to me and it wasn't the same as owning one. Besides, it had been six months since I had my last "loaner" and I was getting itchy. The dock behind my house looked very empty and, for a short time, I strongly considered a "billboard yacht", but my itch decided I need a real boat. This time it would be something totally new to me -- nothing fancy -- just a small, simple, fiberglass runabout. I felt that after being involved with scores of boats equipped with such niceties as infinitely adjustable electric mirrors over king-size berths (so you wouldn't miss any of the action) and lead crystal water closets and 4-person Jacuzzi tubs and lobster tanks on the afterdeck, a small, simple boat would actually be a refreshing change. Not being involved with the design for any craft of this ilk (what the hell is "ilk" anyway?) it was evident that I would have to buy one through the traditional route. After years of being in the business, I thought it would be fun sitting on the boat buyer's side of the table. Fun? Little did I know what this would lead to.

So I'm sitting in this boat salesman's office and he's putting the hard sell on me. His white alligator topsiders (with gold tassels) sparkle in the sun and his polka dotted suit, striped bow tie and darting eyes are making me dizzy. Because I think the purchase of a boat of this size and type would hurt my reputation in the big yacht field, I am wearing dark glasses, a wide brimmed hat and I am using an assumed name. Ol' polka dot is moving in for the kill and, this being my first experience buying a new boat, I am becoming increasingly nervous. Polka dot is showing me a small pile of fiberglass junk for which he is asking "only $19,999.99". 20,000 American dollars! My mind started reeling. I thought of the fully equipped mahogany and oak cruisers I had purchased in the past for far less money. And these boats were <u>still</u> available for less than $20,000! Visions of glistening varnished bright work and beautiful chrome plated bronze castings slipped through my mind's eye as I said to myself -- "what the hell am I doing here? Can I really own a boat like this?" After lying dormant for five years, an old feeling was coming over me! It was happening again and I couldn't help myself. It started with a twinge in the stomach and a tightening of the muscle. When I started shaking uncontrollably and sweating profusely, I knew I needed... A FIX! I left ol' polka dot in the middle of a demonstration on how to use a drink holder that was conveniently positioned next to the helm station and ran to my car. I really don't remember driving home, but the next thing I knew I was in my house standing at the foot of the stairway leading upstairs. I NEEDED FIX! I knew that salvation lay hidden in the closet of the back room upstairs. I tried to resist. I clung to the banister but was inexorably drawn up the steps to that terrible room. I remember thinking to myself what a shame it was that after all these years of doing so well, that I was, again, reduced to this. I was now standing in the terrible room before the closet, fighting my craving. I tried to leave, but it was no use and, unable to contain myself any longer, I flung the closet door open and feverishly started to sift through its contents. This closet contained my prized collection of Rudder Magazines -- all the issues from its inception in the early 1900's to its demise in the '60's. I was frantic now, sifting through the piles of magazines, tossing unwanted issues aside until I came to a special one I knew all too well. I was shaking so hard the printing on the pages was a blur as I frantically flipped the pages. And there it was! The top of the page read "PRESENTING THE BRILLIANT 1947 ELCO FLEET FEATURING FIVE GREAT NEW MODELS – 27' TO 62'... FLASHING SPEEDS... NEW STREAMLINED BEAUTY... SENSATIONAL PERFORMANCE... LUXURIOUS COMFORT..." Below was a color rendering of a beautiful 35' Elco Cruisette skimming the surface of the water on a hazy blue day. There were blond beautiful people in the cockpit waving to equally beautiful people on the dock. Fat, pink clouds hung in the sky. Then there was the "kicker" at the bottom of the page... the thing that always made post-war Elcos so irresistible to me. It said "PT PROVEN EIGHT TIMES AROUND THE WORLD. REVOLUTIONARY ADVANCEMENTS FEATURED IN THE 1947 ELCO CRUISERS AND MOTOR YACHTS HAVE BEEN DEVELOPED DURING MORE THAT 200,000 MILES OF SPEED AND PERFORMANCE TRIALS ON THE SAME ELCO PT'S." Wow! PT proven for 200,000 miles! Next to that caption was a photo of an 80' Elco PT boat jumping a wake and looking like it could take on the whole Rising Sun navy single handedly!

    Talk about ads! That ad grabbed me when I was six years old in 1947 and it continues working today. How could <u>anybody</u> possibly resist this? I forced myself to close the magazine but I knew this was not the end of it. Reading that ad again after five long years brought back a flood of memories and I knew that, this time, I would have to go through a long, painful withdrawal to once and for all rid myself of the Elco on my back. You see, my last boat was a beautiful, original, 40 foot, 1946 Elco and boat before that was an equally beautiful 35 foot 1947 Elco and... I CAN'T GO ON. I am emotionally drained.

July 1985

Confessions – Part 2

POST WAR ELCO'S! I had suppressed the thought of these vessels for years, but upon seeing that great 1947 ad I was hooked all over again.

I have a pretty good collection of post war Elco stuff intentionally hidden in various, hard to get at locations around the house so that I would not have ready access to them. After that ad, I needed more. First, I read through the Owner's manual that came with my 35 footer, after which I had a look at some vintage Elco wiring schematics. Then I went down into the garage and stood in front of the Sacred Crate. I had not been through this crate for over ten years. With a crow bar, I slowly pried open the lid and... THERE IT ALL WAS! A box <u>chock</u> <u>full</u> of 1947 Elco hardware! There! Laying on top was the famous Elco script transom ventilator. And over there! Two complete instrument panels. In the corner lay a pile of "clamshell" vents partially covering a pair of shift levers. I grabbed a heavy, chrome plated fuel filler cap (with the Elco script carved into it) and stuck it in my pocket. Feeling much better now, I closed the lid and went back into the house. I sat down, took a long deep breath and it all came back in a flash of Elco vignettes.

I remembered spending every weekend fanatically pouring through the classified ads in the New York Times and Soundings looking for Elcos for sale and making crazy jaunts all over the area to look at boats which I couldn't afford and/or didn't need. I once spent an entire cold, sub-freezing Rhode Island January day stripping hardware off a 35' Cruisette. I wasn't stealing the hardware (though, in the state I was in at the time, I probably would have). The owner of the yard owed me some money and allowed me to strip the deteriorating hulk for compensation (that's where the Sacred Crate of parts came from). Then there was the time I took a winter vacation in Ft. Lauderdale (I lived in Connecticut at the time) and spent my entire week ogling a 47' 1947 Elco named "Snafoo" which was berthed at Bahia Mar. Just before I was to fly back, I couldn't resist making the owner an offer, though again, I couldn't afford it and I certainly didn't need a 47' cruiser at the time. At one time I owned two Elcos and had a deposit on a third! I became a charter member of the Port Elco Club and remember participating in a fantastic Elco parade up the Connecticut River to pay tribute to Elco's past president, Irwin Chase, who received the vessels at his dock on the river. One can see why, after all this craziness, I contemplated the formation of a group called Elcoholics Anonymous for others in my sad predicament.

Then, in 1965 there was the supreme Elco craziness, I actually went to work for Elco. It's true, they were no longer in Bayonne, New Jersey but in Groton, Connecticut, and, they no longer made pleasure boats, only submarines, but the fact is it <u>was</u> Electric Boat Company! I stayed there for over ten years and, more than once, I can remember confronting my superiors with my great idea to bring Elco back into the patrol boat business (with, of course, yours truly as the chief designer). Needless to say, they never thought much of my idea.

Finally a scene -- a turning point in my life really-- came back to me. It was my first encounter with an actual living, breathing Elco (a brand new 35' Cruisette). It happened in Northport Harbor, Long Island, New York, at the Municipal Dock in 1947. I had already seen the ads, but confronting the actual boat was one of life's magic moments. I was only a little guy of six years old, too young to defend myself from the Elco siren song. Not only can I remember what dock she was secured to, but I can remember the tide height and in what direction it was heading. Adult-type people don't think that kids understand art and beauty. They do. I walked in little six year old steps up and down the length of the boat taking it all in. It was taken for granted, even at that time, that someday I would own one. But there was something stronger. Not only would I have to own one but I knew, even at that tender age, that owning one would simply never be enough. Anyone with some money and not too much sense could <u>own</u> one. No, someday I would have to <u>create</u> a vessel as beautiful as this one. That, friends, is exactly when my career in yacht design started. Life takes strange twists and you either have to be very lucky, very crazy -- or a bit of both -- to see your little boy dreams come true. I would venture to guess that most of the six year old would-be baseball players, firemen and pilots of 1947 are, today, snuff testers or Mr. Goodwrenches or foot doctors or drug runners. One needs a very strong incentive to pursue one's dreams.

What was it about the post war Elcos that made them so appealing? Well, in my opinion, it was a number of things. Some tangible -- some not. Certainly the patrol boat heritage had something to do with it. These cruisers were little more than scaled down Elco PT boats built, for a very short time after the war, from 1946 through 1949. Using mostly expensive, leftover government mil-spec PT boat materials, they were of a higher caliber than most production boats of their day. But mostly it was the shapes. Post war Elcos looked like no other boat with their sensuous "S" shaped sheers, low silhouettes, clipper bows, high chined entries and turtle-backed superstructures. Then there were the windshields -- strangely upswept towards the center. And the hardware! Beautiful custom pieces of chrome plated bronze and stainless steel (that, by the way, thanks to Uncle Sam, <u>never</u> rusted). As one scanned the vessel from bow to stern, one would first see the beautiful art deco sculpted stemhead fitting at the bow. Then the streamlined forward cleat, and the aluminum hatch or hatches on the foredeck (which were exact replicas of the PT boat hatches) would catch one's eye along with the beautifully proportioned half-height stainless steel railings supported by custom cast stanchions. The cabin itself had some very interesting metal and wooden window moldings and a series of ventilators set on the window divider. Aft, at the transom, were the famous Elco script vents and custom exhaust pipes.

There was also innovation in engineering. These were some of the first large production boats to employ V-drives with engines located in the extreme stern. This not only made for outstanding accessibility to the engines but allowed all tankage to be installed midships under the salon. Placement of the engines aft allowed a very low silhouette since the deckhouse did not have to be built atop the engines. Construction of African mahogany and oak employed a laminated mahogany stem, double diagonal mahogany bottom planking and batten seam topsides. The boats were rather light and handled wonderfully at sea with their rather deep forefoots, high chines and flat afterbody.

After thinking hard again about Elcos after so many years, a wonderful thing happened: the realization hit me that, while I still loved these boats, I really didn't want to <u>own</u> one again! It was kind of like thinking about an ex-wife. There were some good times but you certainly wouldn't marry her again! I was now at a point where I could think about Elcos but not crave them. I <u>was</u> cured! Now I could reconsider that new fiberglass runabout.

So I'm back in the boat sales office with a new attitude toward the fiberglass pile of junk. The boat salesman, ol' polka dot, figures he has a sure thing this time. I decided that I would give this little boat a thorough, unbiased professional survey. The "hydro-tetra escalator liftoplane hull" looks okay despite the name. As I grab the windshield to hoist myself aboard, it comes apart in my hand (salesman says it's designed to "break away"). Once I do get inside, I am horrified to see that the entire interior is covered with fuzzy stuff that looks like mouse fur glued to whatever is underneath (salesman says beer won't stain it). The deck hardware appears to be made from compressed chicken manure (salesman says he's been wondering what that smell was). The upholstery is copied from a 1957 Buick Skylark convertible (salesman owns one). The portable toilet is located under a seat in the open cockpit. Ol' polka dot is demonstrating how to use it without embarrassing yourself or anybody around you. His advice is to smile and keep talking throughout the entire process. Polka dot is telling me the boat will do 70 mph and is capable of crossing the Atlantic. He is telling me this is absolutely the last boat of this type available for the next 48 months and the prices will double shortly and the new models won't be as nice as this and the interest rates will be going up and he'll offer a special price only for me and wouldn't it be nice to be barreling around the river on a beautiful day like this. He is following me around in lock step with contract in hand and pen at the ready.

After my Elco relapse, I am in a weakened condition and vulnerable. For a brief, fleeting minute I decide that the ideal solution would be to recreate my favorite Elco in fiberglass. Yes, that's it! Fiberglass Elco replicas! I can find this old Elco see, turn it upside down, fair it and pull molds off it. Once the fiberglass shell is complete, I can recreate an Elco interior using all the drawers, cabinets, berths, etc., that I have saved over the years. Then I can have all the hardware replated and mounted on the boat and then...

The contract is on the desk in front of me and the pen is in my hand poised over the dotted line. Did I buy it?.....I'll never tell.

August 1985

Bring Back the Commuter

There you are! Hanging on the handle of the downtown BMT on the infamous New York Subway System. It's August and, as usual, the air conditioning isn't working in your car. You are grimy and sweaty and your $350 hat is limp and drooping over your eyes. Your $400 Gucci loafers are filled with sweat and your $800 blue pinstriped suit (which was neatly pressed when you left your Long Island house this morning) now looks like a pair of painter's coveralls. You are pressed into the car like a bunch of asparagus spears in a jar. On one side of you is an unkempt guy wearing a baseball hat and red high heeled shoes. He is breathing hard, smiling weirdly, and grabbing your leg. Odors emanating from both ends of the fat guy on the other side of you suggest that he recently gorged himself on garlic bread, pickled eggs and baked beans. Your surroundings are hot, very noisy, lurching, jerking, and generally nerve racking. The inside and outside of your train is decorated in abundant graffiti with great sayings like "Jesus is the Conductor of my Train" or "Pedro loves Juan" or, perhaps, the two words that best sum up your feelings about commuting...."Subways Suck." When you bought your beautiful waterfront house in Glen Cove, Long Island, you knew that you would have to travel to work on Wall Street. You would become... A COMMUTER. Commuting in the context of today's lifestyle entails clutching a pole in a long, narrow coffin hurdling through dark subterranean holes in the ground, or driving (or being driven) in a motor car through traffic jams and potholed streets. But it wasn't always this way...

It is 1925. Cleanly slicing the blue-green waters of Long Island Sound comes along, sleek 65' motor craft traveling at 34 mph. The crew, in starched whites, smartly pilots the craft from a low, swept back bridge while the owner sits aft in the covered cockpit enjoying the ride, the fresh air, his Wall Street Journal and coffee and croissants. THIS IS COMMUTING!

In New York City during the '20's, poor and middle class folks clustered closely around downtown areas and took a trolley or subway or bus to work. Nobody considered this "commuting," but simply "going to work" (at this time personal cars for the masses were not common). Only the well-heeled could afford to travel from locations distant from the city. Most did it by chauffeured automobile, however, roads at that time were not very good and the trip was long and tedious -- especially in the summers before the advent of automobile air conditioning. Most of these travelers lived on or near Long Island Sound and many of them owned crewed motoryachts. Sometime between 1900 and 1910 a few pioneering Wall Streeters decided to commute the 26 miles or so down Long Island Sound to Wall Street in their yachts, which were docked or anchored off Wall Street awaiting the return trip later in the day. These first "commuter boats" were merely motoryachts pressed into commuting service but, as time went by, a special breed of powerboat evolved which was known as the "Commuter," or "Commuterboat." By the mid 1920's, a typical commuter was a long, skinny, round bilged, wooden powercraft about 65' long. Her profile was rakish and she was lightly built and powered with huge gasoline engines, usually adapted from aircraft engines of the day. The morning "race" to work was indeed just that: it was not uncommon for these vessels to race one another down Long Island Sound to Wall Street. The fastest boats were held in high esteem and it was not unusual for owners of slower boats to repower them over the winter or to build entirely new boats every few years to stay out in front of the pack. Some of these craft did 50 mph!

A typical morning for a Wall Street executive in the '20's would be thus: our man would awaken late, yawn, stretch, scratch, etc., throw on his bathrobe and slippers, maybe kiss his wife and kids and shuffle down the rolling green lawn of his Glen Cove estate to the dock. His white-clad crew would be standing by and, as he stepped aboard, the already warmed up engines would roar to life and the lines would be cast off. He would retire to the owner's stateroom and, by the time he stepped into the shower, he was already underway at 30 knots heading west down Long Island Sound towards Manhattan. By the time he was off Throggs Neck, our showered and shaved executive would be mixing cream in his breakfast coffee. Breakfast would be enjoyed while places like Beechhurst, College Point and South Beach (now LaGuardia Airport) streamed by. Sliding through Hell Gate, he would, again, retire to his stateroom where, waiting on a wooden stand, would be his suit, shirt and tie. As they approached Wall Street, slipping under the Brooklyn Bridge, our magnificently attired executive would be ready for a day's work after an exhilarating ride of 45 minutes.

Compare the "commuter" described at the head of this article and the one who just stepped off his yacht. One arrives at work hot, sweaty, harried and generally ticked off at the world. This is understandable -- how can anyone arrive at work with a happy attitude when one has just crawled, like a worm, out of a hole in the ground. Our water commuter is fresh and ready to go out and "own the world" (which is just what many of these gentlemen did).

The point of what I am saying here is this: the situation today is very similar to what it was in the '20's (let's hope it doesn't end the same way!). All over this great country we have a large group of overachievers living in high rent districts just outside major cities commuting to work by railroad or in private cars. Many of these guys <u>already</u> own boats which usually have full time crews. Most of the people that I know in this category either drive or are driven to work and back each day and despise it. Their boats and crews are available so... WHY NOT BRING BACK THE COMMUTER?

There are only two requirements for commuting via water to work. They are: a fast boat and a major city accessible via mostly protected waterways from outlying residential communities. A look at the map of the United States clearly shows the major cities accessible via waterway. Boston, Massachusetts; Providence; Rhode Island, New York, New York (where commuter boats were born); Baltimore, Maryland; Norfolk, Virginia; Charleston, South Carolina; Miami and Tampa/St. Pete, Florida; New Orleans; Louisiana; and San Francisco, California are all logical commuting areas. Of course, further north Seattle, Washington, and Vancouver, B.C., look good except for the very short seasons. And let's not forget another great hot spot of commuting during the 20's -- the Great Lakes area. Here we have cities like Cleveland, Detroit, Toledo, Milwaukee, and, of course, Chicago, all accessible from the Lakes.

Although virtually any vessel can be used as a commuter boat, there are some requisites for the ideal vessel. Firstly, she should be <u>fast</u> in order that commuting times via water are equal to or less than those by land. We're talking about cruising speeds of 20 to 30 knots (23 to 34 mph). And because there aren't many Rockefellers or Vanderbuilts or Whitneys left, she should also be rather fuel efficient. These two criteria have already eliminated 95% of all existing vessels. Then, proper accommodations should be fitted, including an owner's stateroom, salon, crews quarters and an open or enclosed cockpit. We are talking boats with a minimum length of 50' and, ideally, 60' or 65'. High speed and efficiency will require lightweight construction and sophisticated underwater shapes. Ideally, a small office should be fitted or a "convertible" area of the salon should include an office. By means of today's sophisticated cellular communications systems and computerization it is not far-fetched to imagine our executive playing hooky on Fridays, while doing his office work aboard. If the idea catches on, a whole <u>new</u> breed of yacht may be born -- dual purpose vessels such as commuter/sportsfisherman or commuter/motor yachts.

But isn't it expensive to commute by boat? The answer is that it is expense to commute by <u>any</u> means-- auto, train or boat. Using the legendary Glen Cove, Long Island to Wall Street, New York run of 26 statute miles as an example, let us investigate costs. Below is a chart for vessels of different speeds and efficiencies. You might ask why dockage in the city has not been included. Since waterfront property is so scarce and expensive in metropolitan areas, I have assumed that our modern day commuter boats would be anchored or moored.

<u>Cruising Speed</u>	<u>Fuel Usage</u>	<u>Round Trip Distance</u>	<u>One Way Commuting Time</u>	<u>Fuel Costs</u>
20 knots (23.0 mph)	1.5 mpg	52 miles	1 hour 8 min.	$45
25 knots (28.8 mph)	1.0 mpg	52 miles	54 min.	$68
30 knots (34.5 mph)	0.6 mpg	52 miles	46 min.	$113

But wait! These are only <u>fuel</u> costs. What about the other costs involved in running a boat? Well, it is my view that, other than <u>minuteman missiles</u>, pleasure boats are the most <u>underutilized</u> vehicles in the world! The owners are paying for maintenance, upkeep and crews whether the boats are being used or not. As far as wear and tear is concerned, I feel the boats would actually <u>benefit</u> from increased use since idleness is the nemesis of marine machinery and electronics.

Now let's look at what it takes to make the same trip from Glen Cove to Wall Street, by automobile, a distance of about 60 miles. Assuming our overachieving commuter is not driving a Volkswagen Rabbit, but a car more suitable to his station in life, like a 500 Mercedes, Maserati Quattroporte, Cadillac Limo or Ferrari 308, we can safely say that he may attain a "stop and go" average of 8 mpg for the hour and a half it would take him to reach his destination. These basic costs are as follows:

Fuel, Wear & Tear at $.30/mile	= $18.00
Parking	= $12.00
Tolls	= <u>$ 2.00</u>
Cost Per Day	= $32.00

On the face of it, commuting by car is much cheaper -- until one considers the <u>time</u> involved. To the high pressure executive, time is money, and assuming that their time is worth $250 an hour, the hour and a half treck by car will add $375 to the cost of the trip totaling $407.00. Adding time in transit to the slowest boat (20K) totals $327.50 and the fastest boat only $305.00 per day, thereby rendering commuting by water considerably cheaper than going by car.

But there is more to it than cold figures. Driving an hour and a half by car from Glen Cove to Wall Street is a harrowing and dangerous experience. The majority of the distance must be traveled on the infamous Long Island Expressway -- the world's largest parking lot. Then there are the toll booths at the Queens/Midtown Tunnel. Here, you might be breathalyzed by one of New York's finest, or mugged, while waiting in long lines to pay your toll. Entering the Queens/Midtown Tunnel is like entering hell. It seems you are <u>always</u> behind a dirty diesel bus belching black noxious fumes directly into the air intake of your car. Once you have made it under the East River, there is still the drive downtown which must be accomplished by taking any one of the main downtown arteries or the FDR drive (it is rumored, by the way, that potholes on this road have swallowed <u>whole</u> cars -- their drivers never to be heard from again). By the time you arrive at Wall Street, you feel like a combat veteran. Your car, which was pristine when you started, looks like an off-road vehicle which has just competed at Baja. With the air conditioning on full blast, you will <u>still</u> be hot and grimy. Of course, your daily exposure on these roads greatly increases your chance of being involved in a fender bender -- or worse.

We haven't even addressed the business advantages of having your yacht near your office. Think of it! Lunches aboard while cruising the skyline. A private haven for a quick nap (or a quick whatever) in the afternoon. Business lunches and meetings aboard will, most likely, provide tax advantages.

A few years ago, on a delivery trip, from South Florida to Glen Cove, New York, aboard a 44' Midnight Lace, we recreated the classic commuter run from Wall Street. We encountered no debris in the East Fiver, the infamous Hell Gate was no problem and we weren't breathalyzed <u>once</u>! Cruising the shoreline of Manhattan at over 20 knots while observing the crush of traffic ashore was great fun. The run was accomplished in a bit over an hour⁻. Think about it, high-rollers and take your choice: the romance of sweet, crisp sea air and sunshine at 30 knots or garlic breath, rotten eggs and diesel particulates. I'll take romance!

September 1985

Triple Screws for the Masses

Back in the early fifties when Chris Crafts were parked in Marinas like Hatteras are today, the hot set up in a Motor Yacht, the ne-plus ultra of the Marina crowd was <u>not</u> a filigreed Grebe, a fine bowed Trumpy or even a macho grey-on-grey Huckins. No, it was a <u>Chris Craft</u> for god sake!

Not just <u>any</u> Chris Craft, mind you but a 51 foot Chris Craft Catalina with THREE ENGINES! THE FIRST TRIPLE SCREWS FOR THE MASSES! The ultimate in one upmanship at the Marina! <u>Anybody</u> could have a twin screw boat, but this was something to be coveted. Yes, triple screws with all the accoutrements: <u>three</u> brooding exhaust pipes in the transom (although the designers never got <u>that</u> quite right with two pipes on one side and one on the other); <u>three</u> beautifully chromed shift levers and <u>three</u> equally beautiful throttle controls; <u>three</u> sets of engine gauges and <u>three</u> ignition keys! This was a real marketing coup by Chris Craft. How could anybody resist the lure of starting three engines in sequence (brooom... broom ...broom) and maneuvering around the docks with three shift levers and throttle controls? Top speeds were rumored to be over 30 miles per hour even though the boats were powered by three Hercules blocked Chris Craft gasoline engines of only 160 hp. each. This may sound anemic for a 51 footer by today's standards, but, remember, back then boats were narrower and light-unladen by the "comforts of home" commonly heaped on today's yachts.

I was just a kid and really into the new boat scene. My dad owned a 1932 Wheeler and my uncles and cousin who cruised with us, all owned boats from the 30's. But old boats didn't interest me much. I was completely taken by the fastest, newest and latest chrome and varnish vessels of the period; the level riding Matthews, Richardsons, Colonials, the lovely Wheelers, and of course Chris Crafts -- <u>especially</u> Chris Crafts and especially the triple screw Catalina. To my mind, this boat had it all. She was beautiful but, most importantly, she was <u>FAST</u>.

Chris Crafts of that era were really something special. Atop their rather prosaic, flat bottom hulls, were set beautifully rounded superstructures with some of the best joiner work ever seen on a production boat. Supplementing the effect was the hardware – custom cast chrome bronze pieces liberally sprinkled throughout the boat. The bows had a distinctive "bullnose" -- with the stemhead well rounded and faired into massive rounded toe rails. The sheerlines, were rather straight but incorporated rounded steps in nearly all models. The transoms were beautiful curved, raked affairs. Then there was the varnish! Above the sheerline, nearly everything was varnish including, in many cases, the main deck which was available in varnished mahogany.

Back then, boats looked bigger than they do today. This was <u>not</u> because I was looking at things from a kid's perspective. Even today, old Chris Crafts look big for their length. Back then, a 50 footer was a <u>big</u> boat! The reason was that the bows had little overhang or rake thus rendering the hull itself longer and giving it more mass. Most importantly, the boats were <u>low</u>. Today, level upon level of accommodations is heaped upon one another to increase living space thus producing a vessel that looks something like a watermelon. In the 50's a fifty-one ft. Chris Craft was, essentially, a single level boat appearing like a big speedboat. Today, most fifty foot Motor Yachts would be <u>triple</u> <u>level</u> boats.

Perhaps the most alluring thing about early fifties Chris Crafts was the <u>exhaust</u> sound. I could write a whole article on this subject alone! Chris Crafts had a very special sound due to the configuration of the exhaust system. Larger models had engines installed well forward resulting in a long exhaust run of large diameter pipe. Part of this long run was <u>uphill</u> resulting in an exhaust which, at idle, delivered water at great gushing spurts interspersed with a long pipe throaty rumble. Fifties Chris Craft exhausts were definitely a piece of work.

As caught up in modern boats as I was, I was reluctant when offered a weekend job by the Captain of an old 62 foot commuter boat named "Go-Go." "Go-Go" was built in 1923 and was over thirty years old. Thirty years old! I didn't want to have anything to do with her, but accepted the post because I needed spending money and liked the captain. He would pick me up Saturday mornings and we would drive to City Island, New York, where "Go-Go" was laid up at Minniford Yard. I would scrape, varnish, do engine work and sand teak. "Go-Go's" long, skinny round hull and squared superstructure looked pitifully obsolete compared to the sleek Chris Crafts that I loved. And the engines! They were the original Speedway 6-cylinder gasoline engines -- massive and heavy, putting out approximately 300-hp each. Each cylinder, the size of a bucket, had its own removable cylinder head. These heads were pulled yearly for decarbonizing. I really thought these slow turning engines were a joke compared to the modern, high speed Chrysler Imperial or Chris Craft Hercules units. I was a little embarrassed to tell my friends what I was doing on the weekends.

"Go-Go" was launched each spring, allowed to "soak up" and then run up Long Island Sound to her home port of Port Jefferson. I was asked if I'd like to ride the old boat up the Sound. Though I would really be embarrassed if anybody saw me aboard, I accepted. So started a Saturday which is permanently etched in my brain.

"Go-Go's" engines, when fired up, sounded like a locomotive. The twelve low speed bucket-sized pistons produced individual, low frequency pulsations that threatened to interfere with your heart rhythm! The engines were controlled from the bridge deck by two humongous shift levers sprouting out of the pilot house sole; each cast bronze and approximately three feet high! This, I thought, was really a joke compared to the tiny round "Chris-o-Matic" shifters recently introduced by Chris Craft. You had to <u>lean</u> on these monsters to engage forward or reverse gear. We smartly backed out of the slip, turned and proceed up Long Island Sound at what seemed like a leisurely pace. After all, the boat was making little or no wake and she was running level. My favorite boats produced mountainous white wakes and stood on their tails. To me, this meant they were going fast. Somewhere off Hempstead Harbor, I spied ahead huge mounds of white foam being pulled by a brand new Chris Craft Catalina. Well, I really couldn't tell it was a Chris Craft Catalina until we were on her quarter because the wall of water completely obscured the boat! As we pulled close alongside, we could observe the owner and his party. It was evident they were the kind of "yachtsmen" that the Captain detested. While he managed "Go-Go" in a professional, almost military manner and considered running a boat serious business, this guy was having a party aboard. The bar was definitely open indicated by the cocktail flag flying from the mast. There was loud music and half-naked women dancing on the bridge. Fenders were hanging over the side as was the boarding ladder. To top it all off, the boat had a very original name like "Betty-Bill" or "Myrtle-George." The owner at the helm, a tall, tanned, trim man glanced over at us and sneered as his hand moved to the throttles. We were close enough alongside that I could see he had <u>three</u> throttles and, sure enough, there were the three exhaust pipes in the transom. This was my dream boat! As Mr. Party-time shoved the throttles forward, the Captain couldn't resist and did the same. We were racing a triple screw Chris Craft! In my heart, I knew what the outcome would be and I began to feel a bit sorry for the Captain who loved his old "Go-Go" so much. Five throttles were put "in the corner". The Chris Craft wallowed, hesitated a minute then slowly picked up speed while sitting on her tail with daylight showing under her forefoot. "Go-Go," on the other hand, accelerated smoothly never changing running attitude. As we quickly slid by the Chris Craft, I looked over at the owner whose ego must certainly have been deflated. Not only was his ego deflated but so was his physique. The tall, trim guy exhaled and turned into a rather short guy with a pot belly! He had had it "sucked in" all this time. His head hung low, he pulled back on the three throttles and turned the music off. In a few minutes, the "Chris" was but a speck on the horizon behind us. I think I felt worse than the owner of the Chris Craft did. A triple screw Chris Craft "blown away" by a 31 year old funny square narrow boat with clunky original engines! How could this happen? Similar occurrences on the remainder of the trip confirmed the fact that the first encounter was no fluke -- "Go-Go" was _fast_.

After that trip, I still liked new Chris Crafts, but it was never really the same again. Maybe there _was_ something to these old boats after all! I started to like my Dad's Wheeler more. When I thought about triple screws, images of three dinged propellers, three buggered strut bearings, three misaligned shafts and, worst of all, three wheezing engines now came to mind. My first introduction into the world of reality! I started realizing there was hunger and pestilence in the world and there were wars going on. I also realized there was something to these old commuter boat hulls and started extensive research on them which led, 20 years later, to the design of the Midnight Laces' which are a throwback to the fast hulls of the 20's and 30's. Yes, that run up Long Island Sound gave me my first inkling that all is not what it appears to be in this world. Later experiences inside and outside the boating world would confirm this.

October 1985

The Fourth Greatest Lie

Since men first set out to sea on logs, there have been three areas in which seamen have always tended to, shall we say, "stretch the truth" a bit. The first has to do with frequency of intimacy with wives/lovers. There is just something about the sea air that makes seamen very boastful about this type of thing. This subject is best left to people like Dr. Ruth and will not be addressed here in any detail (although I reserve the right to do a complete story on this subject sometime in the future). The second topic is their navigational prowess ("Yeah, we set the autopilot at Ambrose Light and never had to touch the thing again until we turned it off in the Straits of Gibraltar"). The third area of boastfulness is HOW FAST ONE'S VESSEL TRAVELS which <u>has</u> to be the <u>fourth</u> greatest lie after: "the check's in the mail," etc., etc.

Speed exaggeration started when a Neanderthal man with a name like "Grunk" straddled a log and rode it with the current down river. That night in the cave while munching Terry Dactyl hors d'oeuvres and drinking jungle vine wine Grunk surely boasted to cavemates about how fast he went down the river on that log (even though the fact was that a few hundred feet offshore Grunk had hit a submerged <u>log</u> and damaged his log!) Columbus, I'm sure, exaggerated the speed of his three sailing vessels to Queen Isabella. This "stretching of the truth" is not limited to ancient peoples. Admirals of modern navies frequently lie about the speeds their ships can attain in order to intimidate the enemy or fund a package through their Government.

And the modern yachtsman... oh the stories we have heard while clustered around the yacht club bar or holed up in the cabin waiting for the weather to blow over! Let's examine some of these stories and analyze them.

"I PASSED BY HIM LIKE HE WAS STANDING STILL."

Fact is that only one or two knots difference in speed when alongside another vessel seems like a <u>great</u> difference. How many times have you overtaken a vessel that appeared but a speck on the horizon? It seems to take a very very long time to overtake this vessel and yet, when alongside, she is passed very quickly making you think that the other vessel must have slowed down. This is the "Nautical Theory of Relativity" in effect which states that: "the apparent speed of the overtaking vessel is inversely proportional to the distance from the overtaken vessel." This theory was first postulated by Dr. Luke Chinewalker in a drunken stupor, who carved it into a Block Island bar counter on July 4th weekend in 1958. (Block Island, by the way, <u>has</u> to have the highest percentage of drunks per square mile on a holiday weekend than any other piece of real estate in the <u>world</u>!).

"WE RAN CIRCLES AROUND HIM."

Translation: The rudder jammed hard over causing the incapacitated vessel to circle another vessel that was trying to render assistance.

"WE WERE GOING SO FAST THE BOAT WAS COMPLETELY OUT OF THE WATER."

This refers to the ride in the travel lift at the boatyard after contact with an underwater object.

If you really want to know your true boat speed, there are a number of techniques available. I ran into one guy in Ft. Lauderdale with a very unique method of gauging speed. It seems he had these <u>calibrated</u> <u>sunglasses</u> which, when he turned his head to the side, would blow off at exactly 35 mph! In discussing a certain boat, this guy told me in all candor that "they said she did 40 mph but I <u>know</u> that wasn't so because my sunglasses stayed on the whole time." Another way to gauge speed is to time the vessel between markers or fixed objects ashore. This is alright except that it requires the use of a stopwatch and a chart to obtain distances. All of this can seriously interfere with partying aboard and is not recommended except for the most serious of yachtsmen. Perhaps the best method of judging one's speed at sea is a system that Captain Slocum used on the "Spray" and is still quite effective today. This traditionally involved throwing a wood chip over the side at the bow and timing how long it took to reach the stern. By knowing the length of your boat, quite an accurate speed could be attained. Of course, this system must be modified for modern times. Since not many boats carry wood chips these days, the contemporary yachtsman could toss a canapé over the side and time <u>it</u>. This is also an excellent way to get rid of an obnoxious guest. Take him up to the bow, explain that you need his help in determining your speed, shove him over the side and time his pleas for help from bow to stern! I know one yachtsman who says he checks his speed with Loran. Well, he doesn't speak too clearly and, actually, he has a leggy blond friend named LOREN who, while underway giggles, coos and shrieks while squeaking in his ear "gee Boopsie, we must be doing 60 mph!"

Boat manufacturers, designers and yacht brokers have been known to exaggerate speed claims. When one is purchasing a boat, he should query the sales people concerning how and under what conditions the claimed speeds were attained. The problem is, there are so many variables. Here are some of the most important:

a) Vessel "Dry" Weight - Weight has a great bearing on speed and can significantly affect it. If you are looking at a 50' sportsfisherman and the broker or manufacturer claims that she does 35 mph, ask him how the vessel was loaded during the trials. Ask questions 1ike: Was the superstructure and interior installed at the time? This is no joke. More than one manufacturer has run speed trials on a bare, empty hull prior to fitting it out so they could advertise a high top speed.

b) Loading - This refers not to the dry weight of the vessel itself but the variable loads that may be carried aboard, which, can drastically affect speeds. It is common to speed-trial boats with empty water tanks and vapor in the fuel tanks. At 7.13 pound per gallon for fuel and 8.35 pounds per gallon for freshwater, these loads can add up quickly. When new boats are sea trialed, they are, of course, usually not sea trialed with owner's gear aboard. This can be a considerable burden, especially if the owner is a weight lifter or is in the lead galoshes business. The weight of gear put aboard has a direct bearing on speeds. Think about it! Dishes, pots, buckshot, cutlery, kitty 1itter boxes, foods, bedding , cases of beer, televisions, washer/dryer, a year's supply of Pepto Bismol, tenders, davits, spare shafts and propellers can increase a vessel's weight by 20% if one is not careful.

c) Depth of Water - It is no secret that fast boats go faster in shallow water. This is due to pressure waves under a fast vessel, bouncing off a shallow bottom and lifting the vessel higher out of the water than she normally would be. One should immediately suspect inflated speeds if a boat was tested in a wading pond.

d) Sea State - Fast boats are faster in a light chop than they are in perfectly calm seas. This is due to choppy waters breaking suction under the bottom and lessening wetted surface.

e) Windage - Windage is not what Uncle Fred gets after he eats beans. This is a technical term referring to wind resistance caused by vessel structure. On really fast boats, aerodynamic superstructures are important for maximum speeds. Tuna towers and outriggers on a 35 mph sportfisherman can reduce its speed by 2 or 3 mph. A large dinghy on the foredeck could be worth 1 mph and an enclosed bridge another 2 mph. Add enough stuff topside and your sportfisherman becomes a poorly performing sail boat!

f) Bottom Finish - A glass-smooth bottom will be

considerably faster than one fouled with weeds and barnacles. Super slick, high-gloss gel coat will be faster than one with bottom paint applied and, remember, everyday your vessel is in the water the bottom is getting more fouled and speeds are being reduced.

g) Ambient Temperature - Cold water increases propeller efficiency and cold air increases horsepower.

From a boat seller's standpoint, therefore, the ideal sea trial is conducted on a stripped hull, with a teacup full of fuel in choppy water deep enough so the propellers won't touch bottom with an epoxy gloss bottom paint job on a subfreezing day in January. From a boat buyer's point of view, of course, the ideal sea trial would be on a fully loaded boat in deep water with a slightly fouled bottom on a hot summer afternoon with fat Aunt Martha sitting at the bow. And remember... don't forget your calibrated sunglasses.

November 1985

Transom Pollution

Many people might think transom pollution is the black and gray stuff that comes out exhaust pipes. Not true. Today our waterways are being terribly polluted by something more insidious -- an affront to the senses and to our intelligence -- BAD BOAT NAMES.

There it was, sitting on the blocks in the boatyard with its brightly painted transom facing the road. The boat was a fairly new Bertram 42' Sportsfisherman in the yard, no doubt, for a routine maintenance and bottom painting. I drive by this yard frequently on my way into town and routinely "check it out" for any unusual vessels that might have been dragged up on shore. On this particular trip, all the boats (including the Bertram) were fairly standard fair, but what caught my attention was the <u>name</u> on the Bertram -- a true monument to tackiness. The boat was called "SEA SECTION!" I could just picture this young, upwardly mobile pediatric surgeon and his ex-nurse wife sitting in their BMW 528 sedan trying to come up with an unusual name for their latest acquisition.

This little episode got me thinking about all the boat names, good and bad, I have run across over the years. Basically, boat names fall into four categories: tacky/no class names, "cutsie pie" names, genuinely clever names, and romantic names.

Tacky/no class names abound. Can you believe that I once saw, with my own two beady eyes, a boat called "LET'S EAT?" What kind of person would name his boat "LET'S EAT?" A waiter? A fat guy? The owner of a diner? There are actually a number of muscle boats in South Florida called "WET DREAM" -- now that's base and surely an apt description of the tasteless owners as well. Other tackys? How about "BOTTOM LINE", "DAD'S TOY", "GERITOL ROCKET", "WATER PALACE" and (are you ready for this bad taste fans?) "CYSTO KID" (owned by an urologist, of course. Would you be this guy's patient if you knew his boat was named "CYSTO KID?").

The waterways are abundant with boats emblazoned with "cute" names on their transoms. Many come to mind: "KRAFTS CRAFT" (pretty obvious where that came from), "LIQUID ASSETS", MOMMA'S MINK", "CHAPTER 11", "CLAMBOX" and "A SEA/D SEA" (I wonder if this reflects the owner's business or persuasion?).

Truly clever names are a little bit harder to come up with requiring half a brain and a little imagination (which apparently is lacking in the owners of boats with names that fall in the above two categories). Some boat names appear completely ordinary until you get to know something about the owner. Back in the fifties, we cruised with a boat called "TAIL WIND." The dinghy was named "PUT PUT." On the surface, these are complete innocuous names and would normally not cause people to raise (or even twitch) an eyebrow. In this case, the owner was a doctor whose specialization was PROCTOLOGY! Then, "TAIL WIND" and "PUT PUT" take on totally different connotations! How about "ESCAPE" -- another seemingly innocuous name until you read the home port -- "Ossining, N.Y." (where a state prison is located!). I once saw an old, tired sailboat with the name "TSOURIS." "TSOURIS" is a rather nice sounding name – one might think it is a galaxy or a marine organism, but no -- "tsouris" is actually a Yiddish word for "trouble"! What a great name for an old, tired sailboat! There was another sailboat about 24' long whose hull was hogged so badly that "CAMEL BACK" would have been a fitting name for her. Her topsides were streaked with rust and her wooden cabin and hull were slowly turning to tuna fish with every passing year. This boat was called "LIQUID WRENCH"! (Whatever happened to "Liquid Wrench" – a smelly penetrating oil that was truly a boatsman's friend in the '50's). There was a boat from Mystic, Connecticut, named "OPTI" under which was the home port "Mystic" -- clever. There was another called "NANOOK" which brought forth images of

Eskimos in Alaska. Actually the owner was involved in the nuclear submarine program and "Nanook" stood for "non-nuclear." Another old wooden boat was called "XYLA" -- a code word? An anagram? No -- "XYLA" is Greek for "pile of lumber." Finally, a bright work laden thirties-vintage Elco was called "UNVARNISHED TRUTH."

Romantic names are the <u>best</u>. Boating (or yachting) is a very romantic past time. Think about it... cruising uncharted waters... discovering new islands and ports... weathering storms... eating meals at sea and sleeping in a berth. A vessel's name should reflect all of this and, you will find, in most cases that experienced yachtsmen most often have the vessels with the romantic names (there is a reason for this which we will discuss later). Great names like: "SHALIMAR", "RENDEZVOUS", "LION'S WHELP", "CARINTHIA", "FULL CRY", "PARISO", "BLACK KNIGHT", "WILD GOOSE", "FANTASY", "RAINY JUNE", "SEVEN SISTERS", "FASCINATING BITCH", "DIANDRA", and "ANAHETA" will long be remembered.

If you just acquired a boat and are trying to conjure a fitting name here are some tips: I know it's <u>very</u> tempting for a husband and wife to combine their names producing an "original" boat name. Names like "MARBILL", "HILDGEORGE" and "IZZYGERT" simply don't make it and certainly fall into the tacky/no class category. This is probably <u>the</u> most common type of boat name in the world and should definitely be classified as transom pollution. ROMANCE! That's what is needed.

It's funny, the boats with the really <u>good</u> names typically have those names applied to their transom with gold leaf. Cute names are usually <u>painted</u> on the transom. The really <u>bad</u> names are typically affixed to the transom with stick on plastic letters.

There are some large yachts offered for charter which are really being hurt by their names. If you were choosing between two similar yachts for a weeks charter in the South Seas -- one of which was named "Desiree" and the other was named "Auto Parts" -- which would you choose? Can you imagine writing a letter home describing your romantic exploits? "Dear Mom: We have just cruised into the palm lined harbor of Papeete on a moonlit night. A soft, warm breeze carried the sweet aroma of exotic flowers to our beautiful yacht, "AUTO PARTS"...". Big buck megayachts <u>cry</u> for a name that suits their image. All too often, these cries are in vain. There are too many multimillion dollar yachts with names like "COPY MACHINE" or "GALLOSHES" or "TIDY BOWL" or "FAN BELT." All these names are, I suppose, a tribute to the owner's business, which provided them the opportunity to own such magnificent vessels. But come on multimillionaires -- A LITTLE IMAGINATION PLEASE! As the size and cost of a vessel go up so should the quality of the name. A 16'er named "ASBESTOS SHINGLES" can be excused. But a 120' Feadship with the same name is completely inexcusable. Large, expensive yachts with bad names are usually owned by young millionaires to whom success has come quickly -- so quickly that it wasn't very long ago that these guys were running around in 19' Bayliners! The bad names from the Bayliners were rapidly transferred from boat-to-boat as the owner moved up. COME ON HIGH ROLLERS! You wouldn't name your beautiful, only daughter "AUTO PARTS" would you? Well, WOULD YOU? Yeah... maybe you <u>would</u> do that!

A very curious thing is occurring in Italy. It is now "the rage" to name boats with American names. If one doesn't truly understand the language some very strange results can occur, though I am sure in Italian they sound very exotic. Individuals and boat companies apply names like "BIG", "LEADER", "COCAINE", "IDEA" and "MICKEY MOUSE" to their craft.

In the end the boats with the magic names are the ones you will always remember. A good name can enhance a vessel's beauty. Recently we completed a beautiful, large aluminum motor yacht for a gentleman who was in the condiment plastic dispenser business. When name choosing time came, I expected the worst. An easy "out" would have been a name like "KETCHUP DISPENSER" or "BARBEQUE BRUSH," but this man had more class than that. He named her "CAPTIVATOR" -- a beautiful name that says it all. If you have trouble coming up with a name for your six million dollar megayacht or even your 15' Sediment Craft, drop me a line with some information about the vessel and yourself. I'll be glad to suggest a few names. After all it's the least

I can do to help stamp out TRANSOM POLLUTION.

December 1985

Mortadella Memories: Impressions of the Genoa Boat Show

If Genoa was a person, it will be a bum lying in the gutter badly needing a shower and a shave. The City of Genoa is a conglomerate of dirty, dingy piles of old masonry -- not a glass and steel structure to be observed in the entire skyline. You really can't blame Genoa for this -- it being so old and all, but a team of sandblasters set loose in the city could have a field day here cleaning up the buildings (and some of the people). Having "hung out" in Genoa many years ago, first as a cadet, then as a third engineer on the passenger ship Independence, I knew the feel of the city as well as its smells and sounds. Only 20 years of additional dirt, grit and soot has change since I was there last.

Genoa was, in the past, a major city of embarkation for the great trans-Atlantic passenger liners which docked here. Back then, the Independence and Constitution docked regularly here (every week and a half) along with many others. The Michelangelo and her sister ship the Da Vinci (probably <u>the</u> most beautiful cruise ships ever built) made

Genoa their home port. But the cruise liner business has literally "gone south" and, sadly, all that is left are smaller, older passenger ships which embark from Genoa for short Mediterranean cruises (the ill-fated Achille Lauro is one such ship). During the turn of the century, the Genoese built a huge castle-like terminal called the Stazione Maritima (Maritime Station) for loading transoceanic passengers on fancy liners. It is still there, but the Galleria d'Imbarco no. 3 which I knew so well during my Independence days is now locked and dark.

The travel log part of this piece is almost over, but Genoa cannot be addressed by this writer without mentioning Ginny's bar. Back in the 60's Ginny's bar was a major meeting place for Merchant Mariners of the world. Located on Via S. Benedetto Ginny's was a "dive", but a home-away-from-home for many sailors. Ginny was a character who did all right for herself, driving a Maserati and owning a Riva Aquarama speedboat (used to shuttle drunken sailors back to their ships just before sailing time). She was kind of a mother away from home for us cadets (and later junior engineers) seeing to it that we didn't get in too much trouble. On this trip, our dingy hotel was only a short walk from Ginny's and, of course, I had to go back. IT WAS STILL THERE! Same crummy sign hung over the literal hole in the wall of an old building that was cracked and scarred. Going inside was a time warp. There were the same dark alcoves set off to the side of the bar separated by the same seedy beaded curtains. And there was the crummy black bar, caked with many years of paint and the wobbly barstools covered with cracked, sticky vinyl. The place smelled like an old spittoon. My memory served me correctly -- this place <u>was</u> a real dive. It was <u>great</u> to be back! Only the faces had changed and Ginny was nowhere to be found. I wonder what she's doing now.

But the reason for this trip was the 25th Salone Nautico Internazionale, better known as the Genoa Boat Show. Set in the middle of this old crumbling city is an outstanding array of waterborne op art. The show is a place of great contrast: plumb-bowed yacht replicas of fishing boats are displayed adjacent to needle nosed ocean racers. The fact that this major European boat show is held in Genoa is an interesting contrast in itself, looking like a space colony set in Stonehenge. Genoa is, for the most part, a "dry" boat show, but the show area is located on the harbor and all large boats are delivered by water, dragged up on a marine railway and transported to the various buildings. This allows rather large vessels to be displayed, the largest this year being a 105 foot AZ. Also outside was an 86 footer and <u>inside</u> the main hall were at least seven powerboats over 70'! Looking out from the balcony of the big boat pavilion is an astounding sight. Here, one gazes across a veritable sea of radar arches, droop snoots, funny stripes, contorted windows, massive air intakes and rocket ship exhausts. Two Hatteras displayed in this hall looked positively antediluvian. It turns out there were only a few new offerings at the show -- most of the other designs had been around for a while. Debuting in the parking lot was the star of the show -- the Italcraft "M 78", approximately 68' in length and, I am told by the designer, heavily inspired by Ferrari's latest supercar, the Testarossa -- a car whose entire side is one big air intake! Also apparently inspired by the Ferrari were the inflated speed claims for this vessel (Ferrari has long been known to exaggerate top speeds). The Italcraft "M 78" is a cruiser powered by two 1600 horsepower MTU engines and banners proclaimed top speeds of 60 KNOTS! 60 KNOTS! 69 MPH! As a fully fitted out, albeit narrow lightweight cruiser, my calculations show that unless Italcraft has achieved a miracle equaling the parting of the Red Sea, a maximum of 45 knots can be expected. If the 60 knot claim is true, and can be proven to me, I will, (1) be jealous as hell and (2) promise to devote an entire future column on the wonders of this vessel. Until then, I will cover my mouth and giggle when this figure is mentioned. (See November 85 Column "The Fourth Greatest Lie" concerning claims about speeds, especially noting the part concerning manufacturers testing bare, stripped hulls with only engines installed). The Ferrari Testarossa was also the inspiration for a catch-me-jump-me red speed boat called... what else? "Testarossa". About 32' long, she was powered by twin Ferrari flat twelve cylinder, 48 valve, fuel injected Testarossa engines. Imagine pulling your Testarossa speedboat into your marina in, say Higginsport, Ohio: "Hey Iggy... the starboard engine is running rough..."

The overwhelming impression of Italian boats is that there seems to be an air vent/exhaust pipe/chine war going on. Intake vents, exhausts and chines are very important to the Italians and these features are often exaggerated to the point of producing deformed, contorted vessels. One sees huge intake recesses in cabinsides only to find that they are fake -

– existing merely for effect. The exhaust pipes are real enough and the rule seems to be bigger and more impressive the better. Some transoms look like the business end of a Saturn rocket! The Italian-inspired trend of running the exhaust outside the hull and covering them with a huge fiberglass or metal fairing jutting out from the topsides 18" or more seems to be losing favor after, I imagine, hundreds of these beauties have been "cleaned off" during Italian docking maneuvers. Walking around the show, sticking one's head into an exhaust pipe here and a ventilator there produced the impression that the ultimate Italian boat might be a huge sewer pipe painted red, one end of which was grilled for intake air, the other end of which was louvered for exhausts! Chines are another story. The height of one's chines seems to be a sign of masculinity and high, exaggerated chines can be found throughout the show even though, after a certain point, high chines become <u>non-functional</u>. The ultimate goal seems to be to make the chines <u>higher</u> than the hull, maybe terminating at the tip of the flagstaff, or something.

Every variation of the radar arch known to man could be seen at this show, including fiberglass, sheet metal, pipe and wooden creations. One seemed to be fabricated of dried pasta. To my mind, the best boat of the show, hands down, was the "Baglietto" express cruiser. This aluminum vessel, about 42 feet long, bristled with innovative features and will usher in a new era of clean Italian design. I couldn't believe it, but she used my favorite line in the whole world -- the "S" sheer. Long eschewed by the Italians in favor of offshore race "banana" sheer, this was a very refreshing change -- one that was mirrored in a few other boats in the show. True to my prediction, the Italians really are rediscovering curves.

English boat names are the norm here: a company called Fiart (please don't leave out the "i"!) has models called "Thunder", "Leader", "Super", "Arrow", "Summer", "Spring" and "Valiant". Other names noted were "Typhoon Super", "Middle Day", "Top Banana", "DC 10", "Sea Racer" and "Cocaine". "Cocaine" is the model name of a line of boats produced in Italy. The name is proudly emblazoned on the topsides. I guess things must be different in Italy. Can you imagine riding around in South Florida on a boat with "Cocaine" written in bold letters on the topsides?

One of the high points of the Genoa show is the equipment/hardware display area. Here, all kinds of intriguing looking hardware is displayed endlessly in a big, three tiered, round building. Some of this hardware qualifies to be displayed in the Museum of Modern Art. What immediately strikes one is that, apparently, thievery is not a problem here. Manufacturers have on display thousands of little pocket-size chrome and stainless treasures out in the open, none of which are fastened down! Contrast this to U.S. boat shows where similar hardware is bolted to a heavy table which is, in turn, chained to the building.

Displays of every type are housed in three large buildings and the parking lot surrounding them. The size of the show and scope of products boggles the mind. There is a large area reserved for scuba diving equipment, another for marina/condos. There is a retail area and a vast electronics section. Most of the displays are manned by very congenial young ladies. Some of them are quite attractive in their own Anna Magnani, sweaty, hairy kind of way. Genoese women look like they're READY.... there is just something about them that makes them look REALLY READY. (I know all about Genoese women... found out about them as a cadet on a training ship docked in Genoa for a week. Damn near left Genoa a <u>married</u> cadet!). Interspersed between the displays are great food stands -- true oases in the desert of boats. These food stands were another show high point -- they serve the best mortadella-on-roll sandwiches in the world. I had one or two of these spicy beauties washed down with red vino every day. As great as these lunches were, though, they paled in comparison to the dinners. Every dinner was an event consisting of a <u>minimum</u> of four courses. The pasta and desserts, especially the gelato (ice cream) are spectacular. Long remembered will be a dessert of dark Italian chocolate ice cream covered with zabaglione (sort of a thin, spiked custard).

    I spoke at length with an Italian designer who explained to me the philosophy of Italian power yachting. Two things that impressed me were that (1) it was strange to find large motor yachts that did not have separate stall showers, but in situ units installed in the heads which, when used, got everything soaked and (2) that most large power boats had very tiny galleys. He explained to me that in Italy the "thing" to do on a large motor yacht is to race at the fastest possible speed to a little seaport like Portofino, Mediterranean moor and <u>play cards</u> <u>day</u> <u>and</u> <u>night</u>! Meals are eaten in restaurants and most of the owners stay in hotels. Did you get that, wretched excess fans? The main purpose for most of the multimillion dollar motor yachts is to provide a place to play cards. This explained a lot, and at the same time, explained nothing. I realized that understanding the Italian yachting scene would take extensive investigation, but schedules dictated that I move on to Hamburg, Germany, for that city's boat show.

Genoa is a large, old, dirty noisy city populated by raving maniac drivers. The accommodations are poor, one eats way too much, the television is incomprehensible and the airport is a joke. I can't wait to return next year.

January 1986

Thirteen Buildings and 3000 Registered Hookers

Impressions of the Hamburg Boat Show

These Germans think of <u>everything</u>! The placard over the bathtub in my plush room at the Hotel Vier Jahreszeiten (Four Seasons) read "To Call Maid, Pull Cord". Over the sign hung a call cord. I looked for another placard to tell me what to <u>do</u> with the maid once she arrived at my tub, but it was nowhere to be found. Talk about <u>maid service</u>!

Finding myself in Germany, for the Hamburg Boat Show, I experienced many little oddities such as the one described above. Since the Genoa and Hamburg Boat Shows overlap we were able to go from Genoa and catch the opening of the Hamburg show.

If Hamburg was a person it would be a dapper, aristocratic gentleman with a bent to engage in sordid trysts every now and then. Hamburg is a neat, clean orderly city with wide, well laid out thoroughfares on which one wouldn't hesitate to drive. Germans treat us Americans pretty well considering that, not too many years ago, the city was turned into a pile of gravel by the U.S. Air Force. The place is all new, virtually rebuild after World War II, apparently using plans of the original buildings for the place certainly has an "old world" feel about it. Like in Genoa, most buildings are stone but, unlike Genoa, they are <u>clean</u>. The stereotype of Germans obeying orders seems to be correct. A good example of this can be found at any street corner. There are absolutely <u>no</u> jaywalkers in Hamburg. When the two little red pedestrians illuminate in the traffic light, people stop and stand at <u>attention</u> until the lights turn green, even if there are no cars anywhere in sight (this is in great contrast to the Genoese who cross the street anywhere, anytime, without even looking, sometimes stepping over cars, sometimes walking <u>through</u> back seats of gridlocked cars). On Saturday morning there was a huge demonstration through the main streets of Hamburg on the behalf of some labor union. Thousands of people took their Saturday to march with their wives and children in a parade which stretched for miles. Someone in our party speculated that if you put a guy with a drum in public square here, you will have an instant parade. Right smack in the middle of this beautiful, manicured city is an area called the "St. Pauli District" otherwise known as the "sin capital of the world -- the world's greatest red light district!" There are 40,000 daily visitors to the St. Pauli district which boasts 430 bars, clubs and restaurants and 3,000 <u>registered</u> card carrying hookers! The thing that strikes one about this area is that, unlike most other cities where the red light section is in the crummiest, seediest part of town, in Hamburg it is right in the middle of the high rent district! Interspersed with some of the raunchiest clubs in the world are some of Hamburg's finest restaurants with names like The Bistro, La Paloma, King George and Capones. By doing this, if a Hamburg resident meets his neighbor in this red light district they can always tell each other that they came there to have <u>dinner</u>. As I said before, the Germans think of everything!

The Hamburg Boat Show is held in <u>thirteen</u> separate buildings. Why thirteen buildings? Beats me. It would have been a lot simpler and cheaper to build one big building wouldn't it? Chalk it up to the Germans' love of organization and compartmentation. There is no other way I can explain it. Calling this a <u>German</u> boat show is a bit of a misnomer -- there are few, if any, German products displayed here. Actually this is a <u>Northern European</u> boat show with most of the products coming from Scandinavia, England and France. Germanic influence is, however, seen in the boats, equipment and hardware displayed: stern... functional... straightforward... somber... DULL. On the "Fexas Fun-O-Meter Boat Show Scale" reading from zero to ten, I rate this show a minus one -- one place below the Stuart, Florida, Annual Boat Show. Blame it on Genoa. After sampling the spectacular exhibits there, Hamburg was a bit of a letdown. Best way I can describe it is that it was like going from a Bordello to Christian Science Reading Room.

This show was <u>so</u> dull that the hit of the show, as far as I was concerned, was... an ANCHOR! That's right, an ANCHOR for God's sake. No regular anchor this was a <u>flying</u> <u>anchor</u>. Looking somewhat like a swallow in full flight, this anchor is attached to a nylon strap rode which was stowed on a reel. Thrown off the bow or the stern, due to its winged configuration it <u>flies</u> underwater at an angle approximately 30 degrees to the surface thereby "making" its own scope! Just toss the anchor off the bow or stern and it will fly forward or aft <u>on</u> <u>its</u> <u>own</u>! I stood in front of the video tape machine watching the demonstration over and over again, completely captivated by this ingenious device (those of you familiar with this column will probably think this is a gag, but, I promise, it isn't). Even the deck shoes shown here are dull. In Genoa, one could find tri-colored deck shoes in all kinds of leather, satin or fabric with gold sequins on them with or without heels. Decks shoes displayed at the Hamburg Boat Show were big, clunky, clubfooted affairs with soles that looked like <u>gravel</u>! Most of the powerboats shown here are heavy, single engine, low powered jobs with round bilges and semi-displacement hulls. If one were in the market for a double ended powerboat this would be place to shop. Many of the powerboats here may best be described as "tubs". Throughout the show a loudspeaker system wired to all the buildings carries constant announcements in German reminding one of a bad German prisoner of war movie.

 Last month, I spoke about the wonderful Mortadella sandwiches served at the snack bars at the Genoa Boat Show. Here in Hamburg, a raft of very neat, orderly snack bars were sprinkled about the show selling, among other things, very tempting looking bratwurst. So I ask the nice lady for a bratwurst. She asks me if I want it on a roll. I say "yes, of course". She hands me a bratwurst approximately 8" long with two tiny pieces of bread each approximately 1-1/2" in diameter. I pay the lady and take my lunch to a little table. I sit there not knowing how to eat it. Holding the little pieces of bread on either side of the bratwurst reminded me of a snake wearing <u>earmuffs</u>. Not wanting to look like a jerk, I wait for a "local" to order the same thing and watch how he eats it. He picks up the bratwurst and eats it like a celery stalk. I do the same. So much for German lunches.

After three days of mingling with Germans I came to the startling conclusion that Germans must have two languages. One is the language known throughout the world as "German" and is used in day-to-day affairs. The other is, for want of a better term, what I'll call "German bedroom talk" which is only used after hours in the bedroom. I have arrived at this conclusion by deduction -- how could the German race possibly has propagated if "German" was spoken in the boudoir? It just isn't possible. Having sweet, spritzy, guttural German nothing like: "SCHUHE AUSZIEHEN! NICHT RAUCHEN! WARTEN SIE NICHT! JEDER KANN TEILNEHMEN!" whispered in your ear <u>has</u> to be the most unexciting, uninviting thing in the whole world! They simply <u>have</u> to have another language.

Sunday, it was time to go home. I mean it was <u>really</u> time to go home. After cutting short the Annapolis Boat Show to fly to Genoa and, thereafter, directly to Hamburg -- about two weeks of solid boat shows -- the boating part of your brain goes on "overload" and you are beginning to hate boats. When your feet feel like they're attached to your knees and your socks start to creeping down into your shoes with every step and the elastic in your short fails, you know it is time to leave. Time to go home and rest for the Ft. Lauderdale Boat Show, coming up in a week and a half!

I left Germany with only one regret: I sure wish that I had the <u>guts</u> to call the maid when I was in that tub!

February 1986

In a Slump

I admit it. I'm in a <u>writing</u> <u>slump</u>! As this is being written, it is the very beginning of a New Year, I'm just back from a great vacation, my mind is filled with great resolutions but I have absolutely nothing to write about this month. So I think I'll take this opportunity to sign off, wish you all a Happy New Year and see you on these same pages next month.

Come on now! If guys like Dan Marino, Mickey Mantle and Magic Johnson can have slumps why can't I? It's not like I don't have any ideas, it's just that none of them can be developed into a column, for one reason or another. The only good thing that can be said about a writer's slump is that nobody gets hurt. If a doctor has a slump, he could lose patients. When a layer is in a slump, his clients can go to jail. When a druggist is in a slump he can O.D. his customers. But when a <u>writer</u> is in a slump, the worst thing that can happen is <u>bored</u> <u>readers</u> and a <u>disappointed</u> <u>editor</u>, but so be it. I am really sorry to have disappointed you this month, sweet Bonnie, (my understanding editor) and I promise to have a great column for the next issue.

I <u>could</u> have written about airline gates. But airline gates don't really pertain to power boating for most people. In my case they <u>do</u> because I am always flying off somewhere to see this boat or that client or go to some boat show. I don't really fly for any other purpose. Airlines gates have always been an enigma to me. I simply cannot fathom why my gate is ALWAYS THE LAST ONE way down the end of an endless corridor like you'd find in Chicago or Atlanta -- so long that the curvature of the earth obscures the end! When I get a gate number 47 or 52 I expect the worst and prepare for the long haul. What bugs me, however, is that when I get "Gate 1", and I am simply overjoyed at my good fortune, I then find that the corridor <u>STARS</u> <u>OFF</u> WITH GATE 150 AND <u>GATE 1</u> IS WAY DOWN AT THE END! It happens every time! The only thing I can figure is that this is a massive, organized airline conspiracy against me. I can just see Frank Borman at his weekly staff meeting leading off the agenda with something like: "Gentlemen, I see that Fexas is booked on flight 179 to New York, let's make sure his gate is way down the end of the ramp."

I have a column ready entitled "Getting Acquainted with your Stuffing Box", but I am saving that gem for the gala spring stuffing box issue of Power and Motor Yacht.

I thought I would do a column about yachting etiquette and address areas in this field that you don't find in the snooty yacht etiquette books. This would address unusual situations afloat. The prospects for this column were unlimited. "Barfing Over the Side", "Relieving Yourself Over the Stern" and "The Leeward Burp" were but three of the fascinating, useful subjects discussed but I had to scrap the idea since I knew my mother would think I was disgusting (she already suspects this from some of the rotten things I've said in this column in the past) and disown her only son.

I had another great idea for a column based on the popularity of the "Miami Vice" television show. There have been articles on the stars, the clothes, the buildings, the cars, and, of course, the boats. My column was entitled "Bottom Paints of Miami Vice". Leading off with a picture of Don Johnson in his Sergio Armani jacket and silk shirt painting the bottom of his Scarab speedboat pink and pastel blue. It turned out, however, that the producers of the show would not release the info I needed about the bottom paint they use.

Another terrific idea was a piece for the benefit of our women readers. It was titled "A Women's Guide to Topless High Speed Powerboating" subtitled "An Alternate Use for Flopper Stoppers". As great as the idea was, I never pursued it because I knew my editor would give it the ol' black marker and call me a chauvinist.

One idea that had real promise was titled "Famous Sober Yachtsman of the World", but the list was simply <u>too</u> <u>short</u> to develop an article. I then thought I'd go the other way with a story called "Famous Drunken Yachtsmen of the World" but I only needed enough material for a <u>single</u> <u>column</u>, not an <u>entire</u> <u>book</u>!

Let's face it, <u>none</u> of these ideas are any good! I am simply in a slump. When Magic Johnson is in a slump, he goes out in the back yard and shoots baskets. Mickey Mantle went to the ballpark and hit flies to the outfield. But does a writer do when he is in a slump? Jot down the alphabet? Or does he repeatedly copy famous pieces of writing? THAT'S IT... Just the thing to get me in shape for next month's column. Let's see here... Four score and seven years ago....

March 1986

Transom Sewage

The situation is much worse than I thought. When I wrote the "Transom Pollution" piece in the December issue, I attacked the tacky/no class names I have seen on our waterways. Since then, we've been buried in letters from people all over the country submitting names that surpass the tacky/no class classification and solidly move into the "rotten" realm of names -- names even I never would have thought of.

I have always prided myself as being a pretty rotten guy. My qualifications, after all, are impressive. When in college, I formulated a "Rottenness Theorem" which states: "if you put a bunch of stuff (apples, fish, people, etc.) in a confined area and leave them there long enough some rottenness will emerge". I was normal enough until I went to a <u>military college</u> where a bunch of guys were sequestered on a peninsula for <u>four years</u>, paroled only on Sundays. In a situation like this, the rottenness theorem applied and rottenness bred like the cockroaches that adorned the walls of the barracks we lived in (we called it "living wallpaper").

After four years, I had my degree in rottenness. My master in rottenness was attained in the Merchant Marine. There are some truly raunchy people in the Merchant Marine and I learned well during my three year stint. But I advanced to a true virtuoso in rottenness during my years working at a submarine shipyard in Connecticut, predominantly with guys from Rhode Island. Guys from Rhode Island are really bad. Here, the rottenness theorem truly shines. Rhode Island, after all, is a tiny state packed with people and it's been around for hundreds of years. The place is steeped in rottenness.

After all that training and experience, I thought I could hold my own with anybody when it came to rottenness. I am, however, man enough to admit that, even with my impressive credentials, I have been thoroughly outclassed by many boat owners out there. You have already seen some of these dreadful boat names published in the "Mail Drop" section of this magazine and they have inspired some more thoughts on boat names. WARNING: This article contains some really raunchy names. Do not proceed if you are easily offended and do not write me letters of outrage after you have read it. The names mentioned here are real and are in the public domain. I am merely reporting the facts to you, so don't get mad at me.

Ever notice that the boats with the really crummy names are the ones that run over your anchor line in a crowded harbor, or launch their dinghies upside down, or play their Spike Jones records over their hailer in a quiet anchorage, or fly skull and crossbones flags from their masts? This is because boats with bad names are <u>never</u> owned by experienced waterman. They are owned by turkeys and greenhorns (many of them <u>perverted</u> turkeys and greenhorns). My advice is that when a boat with a name like "Ba-Ba-Louie" or "Bug Juice" or "Arm Pit" pulls into your harbor, weigh anchor and leave immediately.

Don't these jerks feel pretty foolish when they have to use their boat names in conversations? Scenario #1: "Mayday, this is the BEARDED CLAM (I didn't make this one up folks and I have a picture to prove it) calling the U.S. Coast Guard, do you read me?" "This is the U.S. Coast Guard, could you spell the name of your vessel please." "Yes, that's B-E-A-R-D-E-D C-L-A-M, do you copy, over? "Yes, I copy but I don't believe it. What is the nature of your problem?" "The BEARDED CLAM is leaking!" (Long pause) "Sir, I don't believe you want the Coast Guard, have you consulted a gynecologist?" Scenario #2: You berth your boat at the posh Ocean Reef Yacht Club in Key Largo and make your way to the dockmaster's office which is filled with professional captains and wealthy yacht owners sitting around telling sea stories. You approach the dockmaster and tell him you want to register. The dockmaster asks the name of your boat. How are you going to feel standing in front of grown men saying to the dockmaster: "Purty Poo"? Scenario #3: You have invested heavily in pork bellies only to find that they have regurgitated, but the transmission on your Ferrari Boxer has turned to ravioli and you need a quick $15,000 to fix it. So you go see your friendly, neighborhood Chase Manhattan banker. You are led into his oak paneled office and he is sitting behind his massive carved mahogany desk with his three piece grey flannel suit, wing-tipped black shoes, white shirt and conservative tie. He is sternly looking over his rimless bifocals at you reminding you of your algebra teacher in high school. "Well, certainly you can use you boats as collateral, sir, all I need is some basic information. First, what is the name of your boat?" Do you think for a minute you'd have a snowball's chance in hell of getting a loan if you told him your boat's name is "Tally Whacker"? I sure doubt it. Scenario #4: You are in the marine store and the guy behind the counter is a surly, burly bloke who looks like a Chicago Bear linebacker. You take your stuff up to the counter and he is writing up the slip. "Boat name?" he asks. "Er... For Q" you say "Well "For Q" too buddy", he says as you are thinking how you will get on and off your boat in a wheelchair. Scenario #5: You are at Walker's Cay in the Bahamas, everyone is partying at the bar and you meet the woman of your dreams. She is a true Goddess in every sense of the word and you are trying hard to impress her. Things look good and, after chatting for a while, you invite her to your boat for a nightcap. "I'd love to" she coos "but I want to let my friends know so they don't worry. Tell me the name of your boat and I'll meet you there." You nuzzle up close and romantically whisper in her shell-like ear: "Hemorrhoid". Needless to say, the magic is gone.

    The fact is that very few people will take you and your boat seriously if it has a really rank name. This not only includes yacht clubs and bankers, but insurance companies, marine repair facilities and bridge tenders. If I were a boatyard owner doing repairs on a boat called "Squid Lips" I think I'd tack 50% or 60% on the bill just for the hell of it. If you were a Coastguardsman and received two distress calls, one from a boat called "Rendezvous" and the other from a boat called "Bow Movement" (sorry, didn't make this one up either folks) and you only had one rescue boat, which one you would respond to first? If you were a dockmaster with one berth available and two boats called in simultaneously looking for a slip for the night, one boat called "Lions Whelp" and the other called "Poverty Sucks" which one would you offer the slip to?

I'm afraid bad taste is here to stay. Some of you out there have been wise enough to respond to my offer to help name my boat. But many others are <u>beyond</u> help and, to tell the truth, I am rather fed up with the whole thing. So, Randi and Sidney, go ahead and name your boat "Ransid"... I don't care. And, Frank and Lynne (with your cute little boy Ben), go ahead and name your boat "Ben Franklyn"... it doesn't matter to me. Your yuppie neighbors at the marina will love it. Barbara and Constantine, you can name your boat "Bacon" and while you are at it name your damn dinghy "Eggs", because I really don't care anymore. You're all beyond help.

I am so disheartened and disgusted with all this that it is time to take drastic action. ARISE YACHTSMEN OF TASTE! REBELL AGAINST THESE CLASSLESS ROGUES WHO POLLUTE OUR WATERS! Join the TFTPO (Tom Fexas Transom Pollution Obliterators). Arm yourself with aerosol paint cans and steal into the night in your dinghies rowing stealth fully from bad boat name to bad boat name, obliterating the plague with black spray paint! BAN TOGETHER, ARISE AND HEAR THE CALL!

April 1986

Magical Miami

If you approach the Miami Beach Convention Center the back way you take a left early off Alton Road, turn left at the light on Dade Boulevard and then hook a quick right over the little bridge on Meridian Avenue. Look at the left and... BAM! The scene hits you by surprise sending your boat mind reeling. There, on the left, are acres of gleaming power boats! Except one doesn't immediately see the boats-- what you first see are striped tents, grandstands, signs, barricades, umbrellas, waving banners, flying balloons, soaring outriggers, reaching antennas and radar arches at all kinds of crazy angles.

When you get a little closer, you can start making out shapes of hulls and superstructures. A maze of powerboats. Every kind of powerboat you ever dreamed of, all in one place, under the warm Florida sun. Powerboat Nirvana! And this is only <u>one</u> of, what are really, <u>five</u> separate boat shows here in Miami. In addition to the outdoor parking lot boat show there is: the indoor coliseum boat show, the Marriot Hotel floating boat show, the Collins Avenue floating boat show and the sailboat floating boat show.

The NMMA did an outstanding job on this show. What brought it all together was their bold, but necessary, step of banishing the ragbaggers to the "Siberian docks". That's right, not a sailboat to be found (other than a few small ones) in the entire boat show!

To a powerboat nut, it's all a little overwhelming -- like a walk through F.A.O. Schwartz at Christmas time when you were five years old. Every type of boat conceived since the dawn of mankind is displayed here. There are row boats, blow boats, peddle boats, metal boats, tug boats, drug boats, funny boats, playboy bunny boats, cat boats, fat boats, day boats, play boats, nice boats, Miami Vice boats, staid boats, rosewood inlaid boats, styrene boats, submarine boats, fast boats, bad ass boats, marsh boats and omigosh boats, gilt boats and never should have been built boats, old fart boats and stop your heart boats, porta boats and don't go near the water boats, clunker boats and Archie Bunker boats. Miami is one of the few boat shows in the world that can truly be called "international". Seen were boats from Canada, Italy, France, Brazil, Sweden, U.K., Taiwan, Red China, Hong Kong, Australia and, of course, the USA.

The best way to see all of the show is with a carefully laid out plan. Usually, I formulate my plans over a great breakfast at "The Original Manny's Restaurant" (as opposed to ... what? Imitation Manny's Restaurants?) Coffee, juice, corn muffins (or toast), two scrambled eggs and three sausages for $3.46. Only a block from the coliseum. You can't beat it. The clientele is mostly retired people. Not surprisingly, the first thing on the menu is prune juice!

Miami, during the boat show, is truly a crazy place. In addition to the five boat shows, there is the Coconut Grove Art Festival and, of course, the Miami Grand Prix, all on the same weekend. For the Grand Prix, most of downtown central Miami is barricaded for the race cars, making getting around a real hassle. But sounds of screaming cars adjacent to the Marriott floating boat show make it all worth it. Miami is a magic city which has been great popularized by the television show "Miami Vice". While driving west along one of Miami's beautiful causeways at night with the skyline glittering in the background and the streetlights reflecting off the hood of your car, you can't help feel like you're Don Johnson blasting along in your shiny black pseudo-Ferrari to make a bust (or, possibly, just to ogle one). But things are never like they are in the movies. You are driving a wheezing Pontiac Sunbird rental car with a bad rear end in bumper to bumper after show traffic. The streetlights are diffused in the dull, scratched, sun bleached bilious green paint of your hood. You have a big mustard stain on your shirt and the tissue paper is still on your face from the shaving cut this morning. Reality is such a letdown! The detours downtown take you through some really seedy parts of the city. Just a few blocks away from the Marriott/Omni glitter palaces, the streets turn to gray, dingy sameness -- dark and empty. Shadowy figures dart in and out your peripheral vision. There are times when you run red lights rather than stop because of the shady characters hanging around. Where are Crockett and Tubbs when you really need them?

Miami Beach... the world's greatest <u>aunt</u> colony. <u>Loaded</u> with retired New Yorkers. With the populous made up predominately of retired folks, observing the scene can be quite interesting. For example, many streets of Miami Beach have remote television cameras mounted at each of the four corners of <u>every</u> intersection for the reason, of course, of deterring crime. How can the cops monitor four cameras at nearly every main intersection in Miami Beach? I don't see how this is possible. I would bet my favorite planimeter that they are empty camera shells placed there solely for peace of mind! Surgical supply stores proliferate and a Burger King or McDonald's is nowhere to be found. The craziness of the boat show lulls you into a sense of security here, but don't be fooled. One out of town exhibitor had his brand new car, packed full of personal possessions, stolen from the municipal parking lot across the street from the Convention Center. While they were waiting for the police to arrive, they observed a couple of parking meter collectors retrieving coins from the parking meters. This would have been okay except these guys were doing it with <u>hack</u> <u>saws</u>!

The Miami Boat Show is so big and so hectic and so lengthy that when it's over you thank heaven that the next major boat show isn't until fall. The magical Miami show is strong enough to carry you through spring and summer without even <u>thinking</u> about another boat show. Crazy boat show time at Miami -- where the memories (and the gas from the great Italian sausage hoagies) will be long remembered. I'll be there next year. Stop by and say "hello".

Just look for the guy with a mustard stain on his shirt.

May 1986

Good Morning Hong Kong

Arriving in Hong Kong is always an extremely exciting experience. I'm not talking about "Oh boy, this is great" exciting but sweaty, palpitate your heart, wet your pants exciting. And it's not because Hong Kong is exotic or romantic or one of the world's greatest business centers. And it's not because of the startling bargains in gold watches, ultra-suede six piece suits, electronic equipment, cameras, etc. No... I mean ARRIVING in Hong Kong is an exciting experience. You see, on the final approach to the airport you come in low off the China Sea almost perpendicular to the coast line. Trouble is, you are headed for a humongous mountain with an ominous red light atop it. As you brace for the impact, the plane hooks a sharp right at the last minute and quickly lands. Now <u>that's</u> exciting!

Our party flew to Hong Kong from San Francisco on a United long range 747. The purpose of the trip was, supposedly, to inspect a brand new 83 motor yacht there with the owners, their captain, their interior designer and their yacht broker. The <u>real</u> purpose of the trip, however, was to buy as many watches, custom tailored suits, cameras, brief cases, jewelry and calculators as possible within the time allotted. In United's "executive class" we were treated the way Frank Purdue treats his chickens -- they keep you confined for a long period of time while continually stuffing you with good food. At the end of the trip, you've had approximately five dinners, six snacks, three breakfasts and four appetizers plus drinks -- not to mention a double feature movie. Long flights are, indeed, a strange set of circumstances. After a sixteen hour flight you are sweaty, irritable, unshaven, sleepy zombie. You have to sit next to the same person for sixteen hours who is usually a leper with bad breath. Hell, when I was married I never sat next to my wife for sixteen hours. Someday trips like this will be as archaic as four day flights across the U.S. in a biplane. We will simply be blasted into orbit and reenter half an hour later and half a world away.

When I am king, I will decree that time zones be abolished throughout the world. This is a confusing and unnecessary system brought about by pettiness amongst countries around the world -- just because they want it to be dark in the nighttime and bright in the day. Forget Greenwich meantime. The world will be using "Stuart, Florida, meantime" (Stuart is my hometown). Under my new system, the time in Stuart will stay just as it is and the rest of the world will adjust their clocks to Stuart meantime. This way, when one travels east or west from Stuart there will never be a time change and Stuart residents will never have to lose any sleep trying to adjust to thirteen hour time differences. At twelve noon in Hong Kong it will be pitch black with a bright, shining moon. This will only serve to enhance Hong Kong's exotic image and be good for tourism there.

But, you say, "this is supposed to be an article about powerboats". Well, since the reason I went to Hong Kong was <u>because</u> of powerboats as far as <u>I</u> am concerned this <u>is</u> a powerboat article. But just to make my editor happy, I will mention a few things about powerboats: shafts, propellers, struts, exhaust pipes, chines, fiberglass, sheerlines, centers of buoyancy, generators, blowers, coamings, carlins, life lines, masts and antennas. That out of the way, I will give you my impressions of Hong Kong.

The hotel rooms are exquisite -- even second rate hotels there are better than the best in the U.S. The wood work in my room at the Sheraton rivaled that aboard many fine yachts. This is in sharp contrast to most hotels in the U.S. where everything seems to be covered in fuzzy fabric that resembles mole fur. Remote controls for lights, radio and TV at bedside, a stocked bar, a heavy terry robe neatly hung on a hanger on the bathroom door (with the belt tied "just so"), a tray in the bathroom full of goodies, comfortable beds and outstanding service. The only thing missing was a sign at the bathtub saying "For Maid Service Pull the Cord", but you can't have everything. Snap on the TV in the morning and there, so help me, is a Chinese version of the "Today Show" complete with an oriental Jane Pauley! That's right, an oriental Jane Pauley replica with a pageboy haircut and a "too sweet to be true at this time in the morning" attitude. The show is called "Good Morning Hong Kong". On my first morning there, the lead headline on the South China Morning

Post (which is slipped under the door at precisely 5:00 a.m. every morning) read in big letters "Night Club Purge in the Cards". Just my luck! So much for my night life in Hong Kong. There are really big problems with the night club trade in Hong Kong, the most serious of which is that many clubs do not abide by the law which says "each seat must face out from the wall and have a view of at least one-half of the dancing area". Things are though all over. The front page of the Hong Kong South China Morning Post is very interesting. While American papers splash headlines of politics, mass murders, muggings, rape, robbery, international terror, etc.... the front page of the Hong Kong paper, in addition to the important night club story, contained the following headlines: "Leak Contaminates 5 Workers", "Cold Snap Hits New Territory", "Fish Farms Fund Plan to Aid Tourists", "Third Time Around for Hail Sham" (Britain's Lord Chancellor, 78 Years Old, Married for the Third Time). And there is always an article concerning the British Commonwealth. Today, it was entitled "Australia Severs Colonial Ties". The gist of this story was that, apparently, some ungrateful Aussie "mooned" the Queen on a recent visit there. The only piece of hard news on the front page stated "Acquino Restores Habeas Corpus". Interesting.

Anyone who loves powercraft will love Hong Kong. The harbor is teeming with various and sundry powercraft. When viewed from the heights of Hong Kong Island, the harbor reminds one of a pond filled with darting water bugs. In the harbor one can see freighters, tankers, passenger ships, hovercraft, launches, ferries, jet powered catamarans, hydrofoils, motor yachts, and, of course, junks and sampans, in a constant state of frantic motion. Cheoy Lee (where we were inspecting the 83) builds an amazing array of powerboats on an island off the coast. They probably build a larger variety of watercraft than any other company in the world. They build (in fiberglass, steel or aluminum) commercial ferries, fast launches, patrol boats, freighters, exotic motor yachts, trawler yachts, tankers, motorsailers, express cruisers and sportsfisherman plus lines of sailboats. This diverse activity makes Cheoy Lee one of the most fascinating boat yards in the world.

Talk about boatsmen! Hong Kong has what is probably the world's most dedicated group of boatsmen in the world. We who use our boats maybe twenty weekends a year are mere wimps in the boating world compared to these people. They are the "boat people" of Hong Kong, living on islands made up of <u>hundreds</u> of junks rafted to one another forming huge "boat people" villages. The story of these people is intriguing. They migrated to Hong Kong from China over a hundred years ago, and, being fishermen, they set up their floating villages in the harbor. These people were the world's ultimate boatsmen of all time, NEVER SETTING FOOT ASHORE DURING THEIR ENTIRE LIFE! In addition to being discriminated against by the "land people", they believed stepping ashore would bring them bad luck so they lived out their lives aboard their crowded junks. You could tell "boat people" by their stature. They were small and frail because they simply didn't have room to move around and exercise. Can you imagine having the topsider concession in a place like this? They had floating places of worship, floating stores, floating schools, floating post offices, etc. Nowadays, the second and third generation boat people <u>do</u> venture ashore for school, shopping, jobs, etc., but still live aboard junks.

Above all, Hong Kong is a place of great contrast. A few hundred yards away from the teeming villages of floating poverty lies the magnificent Aberdeen Yacht Club. Tied behind the club are some of the most luxurious, sleekest yachts in the world. Seen were vessels from Holland, a bunch of Italian rocket ships, many Bertrams and Hatteras' and a number of Cheoy Lees. Put a Riva next to a broken down Chinese junk and you are talking <u>contrast</u>. This is mirrored on the streets of the city. It seems to me four classes of people live in tiny Hong Kong (only 410 square miles including the new territory) and their status in life is reflected by their transportation. The rich drive Rolls Royces. There are "rollers" all over Hong Kong -- 600 of the suckers -- the highest per capita number of Rolls Royces in the world! The total number of Rolls Royces in Hong Kong is the <u>third</u> <u>highest</u> in the <u>world</u> after the U.S. and Saudi Arabia! 1.46 Rolls Royces per square mile! Figuring that two-thirds of Hong Kong is unpopulated new territory, this makes the total 4.43 Rolls Royces per square mile in populated areas! The middle class all seem to drive Mercedes Benz cars -- I've never seen so many Mercedes in one place in my life, Germany notwithstanding. A Mercedes Benz is the Chevy Nova in Hong Kong. Less fortunate folks mostly drive compact Japanese cars and, of course, the poor folks walk or take the bus. The snooty Peninsula Hotel has <u>twelve</u> dark green Rolls Royce sedans shuttling people to and from the airport! Not to be outdone, the Regent Hotel across the street has a fleet of stretch Daimler dark gray, razor back limos to do the same. They drive through streets teeming with pedestrians without regard to life or limb. Just keep our foot down and the hordes will part like a school of minnows making way for a shark.

Of all the wonders of Honk Kong the thing that impressed me most wasn't the posh hotels, the exotic women, fancy cars, the world's longest escalator (up the side of a mountain to an amusement park!), the "Jumbo Floating Restaurant" (which serves 2500 people at one sitting), the frantic harbor nor the floating villages. The thing that impressed me the most was... scaffolding! As an engineer my eye was continually drawn to seemingly haphazard scaffolding erected from bamboo lashed together with rubber straps. You see forty story buildings completely surrounded by bamboo scaffolding made up of short lengths of bamboo, approximately 25 feet long, each tied to the other with a damn rubber strap. After spending a great amount of time studying these contraptions, I came to the conclusion that, other than spiders which spin structurally beautiful webs, Chinese construction workers are the greatest natural engineers in the world. There are no blueprints or instructions for erecting bamboo scaffolding. It is all done by "seat of the pants". Larger diameter bamboo rests on the sidewalks with pieces growing gradually thinner as the height increases. These vertical assemblies support horizontal catwalks also made of lashed bamboo and are placed around every floor of the building. Interspersed with these vertical and horizontal members are diagonal braces or struts lashed across the structure at 45 degrees angles. Think about it -- standing forty stories above the ground on a rig made up of short lengths of lashed bamboo.

Hong Kong does a land office business in luggage. The reason is that, when you are there, you buy so much stuff that you need at least two extra suitcases to bring it all home. To lug back my booty I personally bought a nice, matched set of gray suitcases with rollers and tow straps. In these suitcases I put my seven custom tailored Honk Kong suits (I never wear suits), five ultra-suede sport jackets (I rarely wear sport jackets), twenty shirts, three attaché cases, twenty four watches, six cameras, and thirty two calculators, I really didn't need any of this stuff but it all seemed like a good idea at the time and, after all, that is why we went to Hong Kong.

It is now a well-known fact that in 1993 Hong Kong (which is leased from mainland China -- I wonder what the monthly payment is) will revert back to Red Chinese ownership. The Red Chinese are in for a treat.

June 1986

Where Have All the Steelcraft Gone (Long Time Passing)

Steelcraft! What a great name for a production boat. Let it roll over your tongue a few times. Steelcraft... the images that name evokes. Vault-like security from the ravages of the sea. Your very own little steel ship. Strong, invulnerable, bulletproof. Images of four stack destroyers chasing submarines and cannon shells bouncing off armored topsides. Steelcraft.

Is there anybody out there today who ever <u>heard</u> of a Steelcraft? After World War II, Steelcraft was one of the most, if not the most, prolific boat builders in the world. Steelcrafts were strewn about harbors like so much shredded styrofoam cast upon the waters. Built by Churchward & Company, Inc. of West Haven, Connecticut, they were all over the place -- in harbors up and down the east and west coast of the United States and in the Gulf.

Every now and then a new product comes along that purports to "revolutionize" its respective industry. Steelcraft was one such product. The end of the war in 1946/47 was boom time for the pleasure boat market. After "kicking ass" in Europe and the Far East, servicemen returning home were ready for the good life and Steelcraft was ready for them. At that time, the majority of pleasure boats were built by the time honored "stick and screw" construction process consuming huge amounts of skilled labor and expensive (also becoming hard to find) timber. The fiberglass industry was in its infancy, so, at the time, these steel boats looked like the ideal solution: thrown together with a few sheets of steel -- pressed, creased and bent as necessary, then welded into a one-piece structure. Built just like a car on an assembly line. After all, if steel was good on the Yorktown, it would certainly be great stuff for a 26' cruiser.

The advertising was impressive. Consider yourself a serviceman sitting down with his first pleasure boat magazine since returning home. There, usually within the first ten pages of the magazine, would be a full page Steelcraft ad which must have literally jumped out of the page to the boat hungry buying public of that time. The ads led off bluntly with "Here's why your best buy is Steelcraft". A piece of dock or anchor line encircled nine starred items next to the headline, boasting Steelcraft features. "Lowest price! Safer... With Lifetime Steel Hull! More living space! Dryer... With Sea-Vee hull! Lowest upkeep costs! Lower insurance rates! No dry rot...no worms! Immune to floating logs, rocks! Steelcraft sales and service coast to coast!" It seems exclamation points must have been a big thing back then. Further down the copy seven more exclamation points are to be found. Under the headline was a photo of a cute little bathtub of a boat clipping along on it's obviously air brushed wake. Under the photo was the caption in big, strong letters TWENTY-SIX FEET TWO STATEROOM SEDAN ... $4963.00. That's forty-nine hundred sixty-three dollars folks for a complete, ready to cruise vessel that "sleeps four comfortably in two separate cabins" and includes: "Full galley with refrigerator, sink, and cupboard. Dinette seats forward, big table. Full length clothes locker plus extra storage compartments. Private toilet. Chrysler "Ace" power for quiet, smooth speeds to 26 miles per hour" -- all for $4963.00. The claims went on in the ad. "_More_ room to enjoy life than you will find in far bigger boats! _More_ luxury appointments that make the low price hard to believe! _More_ safety because of the alloy steel hull! _More_ "weatherability" with the fast, dry sea-vee hull design!"

"And remember -- owning a Steelcraft is _always_ a pleasure! Lower upkeep costs -- less maintenance work! No rot -- no worms! Even insurance rates are lower than a wooden boat!" (There are those exclamations again. The ad agency must have gotten a bonus for every exclamation point used in the copy). How could anybody in the small boat market possibly resist this pitch?

She wasn't really pretty. The boat kind of looked like a floating '47 Plymouth that inadvertently rolled into the river. It was all rounded and streamlined with a pronounced "S" sheer line and clumsy bow that looked like a soup ladle. The cabin was extremely low and since the control station was inside, visibility was a bit of a problem, but, hey, who cared. The war was over and it was a full blown cruising boat for

$4963. Besides, owning her would "<u>always</u> be a pleasure" and she had a "lifetime" steel hull that was "immune to floating logs and rocks" (actually the "floating rocks" are easy, it's the ones stuck to the bottom that are a bitch).

It all seemed too good to be true... and it was. The thin skinned hulls drummed terribly, making passengers feel like they were inside a giant Chinese gong, Excedrin headache #37. And the boat got <u>hot</u>. Inside temperatures were unbearable and walking on deck on a hot, sunny day would give present day firewalkers something to think about. Worst of all, after a couple of years the strong, invulnerable, bulletproof vessels showed their Achilles heel. Alas, the "lifetime steel hull" that was immune to rot, worms, floating logs and rocks was <u>not</u> immune to rust. The thin steel sheets, although treated for corrosion, could not withstand the ravages of saltwater and, because the steel was so thin, pinholes would appear in a few years. Maybe they were referring to a <u>butterfly's</u> lifetime. It was not uncommon for one to be able to punch a fist through the rusted hulls. The boats were patched and repatched again until they looked like a quilt, but it was no use. Most ended up a small pile of rust in the back row of boatyards across the country. Another American dream gone awry.

I don't really know how many were sold, but just after the war every harbor had dozens of them. They were built between 1946 and 1951. They advertised monthly in all the boat magazines in 1947 through 1949, but by 1950 the advertising stopped as the rust progressed.

Just last year, while in a taxi in New Zealand between the

airport and Auckland, we passed a number of harbors. As usual I like to "scope out" the boats since I am always looking for new ideas and designs. As we passed by one harbor, I looked, looked again, and then again. I couldn't believe it! There at a mooring was... a Steelcraft! It was like finding a living Brontosaurus Rex in the woods behind your house. A true dinosaur of the marine world happily afloat in New Zealand. Taken by surprise, I grappled for my camera to get a quick shot, but the time had passed. I wondered how many times this lone survivor (possibly the only one in the world) had been reskinned. How many thousands of patches did she have? How many times had her deck burned the skin off the soles of somebody's feet? How many cases of hearing loss were induced by the drumming hull? Sadly, no one will ever know.

Nowadays, when I see and add for things like "lifetime Ginsu knives" or "forever batteries" or "lifetime mufflers", I think of that butterfly.

July 1986

"Sportfishing" Brazilian Style

I could clearly see the headlines of the articles that would appear in the boating magazines: "NAVAL ARCHITECT LOST AT SEA IN DUGOUT CANOE". The boating community will get a good chuckle out of <u>that</u> one I thought as we wildly rolled in the Atlantic Ocean off the coast of Brazil.

Our craft is "Abysmal Tech" -- no more than 2-1/2' wide by about 22' long and fabricated by falling a tree, smoothing up the outside and hollowing out the inside while making both ends a little pointy. I have always been an advocate of long, lean hulls, but this is ridiculous! The wind is blowing between 15 and 20K with 4' to 6' rollers. Aboard the craft is a truly motley crew: two Brazilian friends (a boatbuilder and a yacht equipment smuggler), the "captain", and myself. We are maneuvering around huge, deadly looking rocks that protrude from the boiling ocean surface 3 to 4 miles offshore. Our craft is perpetually sinking. We carry no life jackets, flairs, etc., and, of course, no radiotelephone. As I white knuckle the gunnels thinking about things like center of gravity and righting arms, I reflect (in what I know are my final moments on this earth) on exactly how I got into this situation.

In 1979 I was commissioned by a wealthy Brazilian to design an 85' motor yacht for construction in the south of Brazil. I would make week-long trips every few months to monitor progress of construction. Things went well during the weekdays which I spent at the shop, but when weekends came, my boatbuilder/friend saw fit to keep me from getting bored. One weekend, on my second or third trip, he suggested we spend a bright, warm, sunny Sunday "sportfishing". Sounded good to me -- I'd always heard about the fantastic fishing off the coast of Brazil, a virtually untapped gamefish ground. After about an hour's drive, we pulled into a tiny fishing village on a river and my host proclaimed "we are here". To be honest, I expected to see a tangle of tuna towers, outriggers and antennas on shiny, white Ryboviches, Bertrams and Hatteras. What I saw were a bunch of <u>dugout canoes</u> reposed on mud banks. I told my friend this wasn't much of a joke, but I could see they were serious! We parked and found our "captain", a small, dark villager, built like a fireplug who fished for his livelihood. After formalities were exchanged, the "captain" readied our "sportfisherman" for sea. I really couldn't believe what I was seeing. Our "sportfisherman" was a dugout canoe dragged up on the mud, leaning over its side. She was obviously not a new craft, evident by the wide cracks and checks in her hull (trunk). She was powered by a one lung Japanese diesel which was hand-crank started. This engine drove a skinny shaft through a makeshift stuffing box and a small propeller, aft of which was an outboard-hung rudder with a tiller. The "bilge pump" was a small wooden scoop! Before setting off to sea the "captain" started tearing rags into narrow strips, carefully twisting them "just so" and laying them on the gunnel. I couldn't imagine what this was for, but I surmised it was some type of Brazilian Fisherman Ritual performed before setting off on one's <u>final</u> <u>voyage</u>. Then, the "captain" unscrewed the shaft packing gland and inserted the twisted cloth strips in the stuffing box tightening the gland. <u>MAKESHIFT</u> <u>PACKING</u>! He took the remaining strips and stuffed them into the cracks in the hull. Like I said, "Abysmal Tech".

I weakly protested but was informed that "these fishermen go out in the Atlantic in dugout canoes all the time". The <u>Atlantic</u>! I thought we were <u>river</u> <u>fishing</u>! Although these guys may <u>go</u> <u>out</u> in the Atlantic all the time I wondered just how many <u>come</u> <u>back</u>! As the canoe was slid into the river the "one lunger" was fired up, popping and vibrating. My host proclaimed "this is real adventure, no?" I had to admit this was real adventure, yes. Every few minutes the "captain" pumped bilges with his wooden scoop since the cracks and checks in the hull let in copious volumes of water, even stuffed with rags. Apparently life was cheap in Brazil. We snapped pictures of the craft and ourselves before we left. I thought maybe the camera would be retrieved and the pictures sent to my family so they would know what became of me.

It was right here, at this point that I should have said "sorry guys, have a nice day, I'm going to spend it at the local bar drinking "Brahma Chopp" (local beer) and watching the "G" string bathing suits go by". I didn't. Why? BECAUSE I SIMPLY DIDN'T HAVE THE GOIJEONES TO SAY "NO". I didn't want to look like a wimp. My friends were going so why shouldn't I? Think of all the disasters, personal and global, that could have been avoided if people simply had the guts to say "no". Britain and France could have said "no" to Hitler when he first started his rampages in Europe in the late thirties and avoided World War II. They didn't. The captain of the Titanic upon encountering icebergs could have said "no, we will not maintain speed". He didn't. General Custer could have refused to go to Little Big Horn. He didn't. And Fexas, about to embark on an ocean voyage in a dugout canoe should have said "no", but didn't. Call it machismo, bravado, whatever. It takes <u>real guts</u> to stand up and say "hey guys, this isn't right". It starts when you're a kid and your friends are doing something like sleigh riding behind buses or throwing rocks through neighbors' windows. You go along with it because you don't want to be called "chicken". No matter <u>what</u> the danger.

We set out to sea via a winding river. Upon reaching the inlet, I couldn't believe what lay ahead. We had to negotiate strings of breakers, the likes of which I had never seen before. The wind was offshore and, as one would normally expect, breakers were advancing through the channel perpendicular with the shoreline. What was really interesting was that there was <u>another</u> set of breakers at NINETY DEGREES to the first set generated by some strange sea bottom shape, or, possibly, the devil. This produced <u>very</u>

confused seas. Here was my second chance. I could have said "guys, this is too dangerous, let's go back". I didn't. The "captain" never slowed and leaning on the tiller skillfully negotiated the breakers till we were out in the open Atlantic. The Brazilian summer sun was hot (luckily I had bought a wide brim straw hat). While the Brazilians obliviously fished, I spent my time deciding what I would be in my next life. A baker would be nice, or a cotton stuffer in an aspirin bottling plant or maybe a mountain climber -- anything that would keep me away from the open sea. The day progressed, the unstable vessel rolled violently, the engine popped and bucked, the "captain" scooped the bilge, sandwiches were broken out, some fish were caught and my friends, unsuspecting of disaster, were having a whale of a time.

Luckily for me, our smuggler got too much sun, became ill and requested an early return. His sun stroke was the best news I had all day! We headed for shore. We were so far out you could barely see the coast, but the "captain" knew exactly where the inlet was. Approaching the inlet, I was horrified to see that the surf was much worse than it was when we went out but was comforted by the thought that when we did capsize, I probably could make it to shore. I have to say that our "captain" did a masterful job of negotiating the breakers, waiting for just the right one and riding it in uneventfully. A great showoff seamanship! If this guy could do this in a dugout canoe just think what he could do in a Bertram! Once inside on the calm river, my spirits perked up. WE HAD MADE IT! THERE WOULD BE NO HEADLINES! In fact, it was a real adventure.

One really can't appreciate life without contrast: you must have hardship to appreciate good times. You must have sadness to appreciate happiness. You must have poverty to appreciate wealth. You must experience hunger to appreciate gluttony and you must have voyaged in a dugout canoe on the open ocean to truly appreciate a modern 66' sportsfisherman. Never again I would "bitch" about inoperable microwave ovens, lousy water pressure or scratchy upholstery. It is for this reason that I heartily recommend to all yachtsmen "Sportfishing Brazilian Style!"

August 1986

The Green Icon

The alien space craft careened through the earth's atmosphere on a dark, summer's night. The craft was on a spy mission to observe earthlings and learn about their ways of life. After circling the earth a number of times it observed what appeared to be some type of primitive religious ritual in a northeast city of the United States. It hovered silently over the city with its sensors probing, listening, observing and recording. When it was all over, the alien noted that the ritual lasted <u>four days</u> and concluded that the earthlings must certainly be devout believers to carry on a single ceremony for four days. What they saw was incomprehensible to them.

On the first day, there was a gathering of the devout from all over the land. They converged, some on land and other on the sea, around a huge green icon. On the first night, the icon was shrouded in darkness until, after much chanting, a green beam of light was sent across the water which triggered other lights bathing it in green and red. There was more chanting and explosives were detonated all around the icon. On the second day, more followers arrived and the icon was worshipped from ashore and from small and great floating conveyances. Some of the floating conveyances were modern (by earth standards) but the aliens were puzzled by others that were obviously old fashioned. They assumed this had something to do with some type of ancestor worship. One earthling, obviously very important, was on one of the largest conveyances -- an imposing gray one -- which moved down the river in tribute to the icon. That night many more floating conveyances clustered around the icon and even more people gathered on land. Music played, more chanting was heard and a great shower of explosives was observed -- much greater than that of the night before. On the third and fourth days, hoard of earthlings made pilgrimages to the icon, touching it and observing it close up. Some even entered it (the aliens assumed this was some sort of primitive sacrifice to the icon). The space visitors took notes and made video and audio recordings. When they returned to their home planet an extensive report, maybe even a book would be written, detailing the primitive religious rituals of the earthlings.

With their civilization many thousands of years advanced from ours, the spacemen could never have guessed that this was just a BIG PARTY -- a four day bash celebrating the 100th birthday of a statue -- the Statue of Liberty -- that great green lady in New York Harbor. How things get twisted around when one civilization, believing themselves far superior to another, sits in judgement of the "lower" society! Hell, for all we know Stonehenge was probably just a big barbecue pit where barbarians went to have fun, dance and drink a few grogs! The huge stone statues on Easter Island were probably <u>party</u> <u>decorations</u> for a luau and the pyramids could have been part of a huge <u>amusement</u> <u>park</u>!

The Statue of Liberty was 100 years old. True to the American way (any excuse for a party) millions of people and upwards of <u>40,000</u> vessels converged around her for the first time in two days of the July 4th weekend. One of the greatest armadas of all time consisting of battleships, aircraft carriers, destroyers, tugs, sailing ships and myriad smaller vessels moored together for the <u>world's</u> <u>greatest</u> <u>rendezvous</u> -- a pleasure boat "happening", probably never to be repeated again. The American Broadcasting Company <u>bought</u> this year's July 4th weekend for many millions of dollars. How can a company <u>buy</u> July 4th weekend? I don't understand, but I hear they are now negotiating to buy Christmas and Easter. Anyway, they had exclusive television rights to "Liberty Weekend" and beamed the festivities all over the country and to the four corners of the earth. ABC had many hours of air time to fill. New York local TV and radio stations devoted great chunks of time to the revue. One radio station, WOR, devoted FOUR FULL DAYS, 24 hours a day, to Liberty Weekend. During these four days, TV viewers and listeners were bombarded with Liberty trivia. We learned everything we wanted to know about the statue and many things we didn't want to know. We learned what Liberty's sculptor Frederic Auguste Bartholi ate with his cornflakes in the morning. We learned about the little town in Norway where the cooper ore for Liberty's skin came from. We learned that Liberty's uplifted arm was in a weakened condition. We learned that workmen inscribed their names in the interior stainless steel support structure of the statue, only to have it ordered removed by the statue's inspector. We learned that Liberty's stern visage was inspired by the artist's <u>mother</u>, but that his <u>wife</u> served as model for the remainder of the statue (I am sure this went over big with Mrs. Bartholi: "here dear, put on this robe, hold this torch and put this bag over your head"). The media covered very possible aspect of the statue: how it came about, how it was built, the restoration, the people attending the festivities, the people selling souvenirs and food, the ships and yachts and everything else that remotely related to the statue. By the third day, they were really "scratching" for stories with reporters sent out all over the city to find <u>anybody</u> that had <u>anything</u> interesting to say about <u>anything</u>. Example:

TV Announcer: "the director tells us that Bernie Smith down at the Battery has an interesting person to talk to. Bernie, can you hear me?"

Bernie: "I hear you Bob, this is Bernie Smith down at Battery and I'm talking to Izzy Sloboski from Oshkosh, Wisconsin. Izzy, what are doing here?"

Izzy: "trying to eat this hot dog, Bernie."

Bernie: "Hey, that's a good looking hot dog Izzy."

Izzy: "yeah, it's not bad."

Bernie: "do you usually take it with mustard and relish?"

Izzy: "nah, I usually take it with mustard and <u>sauerkraut</u> but they didn't have any sauerkraut so I thought, what the hell, this is July 4th weekend so I tried some relish."

Bernie: "Ha, ha, ha what a great story. Well, that's it from down here at the Battery. Back to you, Bob."

And so it went for FOUR DAYS. On an all-night radio show, they were interviewing the architectural firm that was commissioned to restore the statue. There was a story about Christy Brinkley and Billy Joel who were on their boat anchored in the harbor. It never ended. By the end of "day three", it was getting a bit tiring.

The thing most people were waiting for was a gigantic fireworks display promised on the evening of July 4th. Great hype surrounded this display. The biggest ever in the United States. This would be televised throughout the country and the world. $750,000 (3/4 of a million bucks folks) worth of fireworks were to be ignited in a short span of 26 minutes. Computers were to synchronize the fireworks with music that would be played during the display. As the skies grew dark, anticipation heightened. By 9:30 people were waiting with bated breath around the country and throughout the world for this fantastic display. The President gave a short speech which ended with "let the celebration begin" as he turned to observe the show. The time that everyone had waited for was here and, indeed, it was a <u>fantastic</u> show of fireworks. Sixteen inch rockets were fired exploding far above the harbor. Forty barges full of fireworks were stationed strategically around the city and fireworks were seen behind the skyline of Manhattan, around the harbor and immediately around the statue. It was truly unbelievable. Unfortunately, about five minutes into this fantastic display, ABC, in its infinite wisdom saw fit to insert <u>commercials</u> -- about five of them at a shot -- at least <u>three times</u> during the short 26 minute spectacular. I couldn't believe what I was seeing. Here was New York City lit up like a birthday cake -- a once in a lifetime pyrotechnics spectacular -- and they were cutting to commercials for people with hairy legs and smelly armpits! There were commercials for cars that drove themselves and makeup and flea spray and some type of soft drink that would instantly turn one into a teenager on the beach. Nice work ABC, you certainly deserve the crass commercialism award of the year for that one.

Saturday we were treated to lifeboat races and a parade of ocean liners. Tall ships and naval vessels were opened to tours. The statue was open to the public and that evening there was an international classic music concert. All of this was duly covered by the media and interspersed with Library vignettes. Sunday was more of the same but included a "sports salute" to the statue, a <u>blimp race</u> of all things, and, of course, the spectacular three hours closing ceremonies featuring 10 million tap dancers, four hundred thousand fiddlers standing on one foot wearing top hats, fifty thousand wriggling Elvis Presley imitators, and a five million voice choir. Waterfalls surrounded the stage and the audience was supplied with reflective gewgaws so the entire stadium was bathed in glitters when viewed from above. Laser lights beamed. Periodically, fireworks spewed from the stage and behind it.

To use and old New York expression… "ENOUGH ALREADY"! Now I am as patriotic as the next guy -- maybe more so. But going into the third day, I was getting a bit "statue weary" and by the end of the fourth day I was completely "statued out". The festivities had special meaning for my dad who immigrated to the United States at the age of 7 in 1910. He first saw the statue over the railing of a steamship entering the harbor, but by day three, even <u>he</u> was getting weary of it all. It was indeed a "glorious 4th" -- the festivities Thursday and Friday were fantastic -- but it should have ended, as far as media coverage was concerned, with the last fireworks on the evening of July 4th. July 5th and 6th were overkill.

To tell you the truth, I was really happy to board the Florida bound Delta jet on Sunday and get away from all the hoopla. Wouldn't you know it! The lady in the seat ahead of me was wearing a cheap, green foam souvenir "Liberty Crown" completely obscuring the movie screen. I'm proud to be an American and I love the statue and all she stands for but ... I think I'll skip the 200th anniversary celebration.

September 1986

Things I Hate

There's a Sarah Lee sing-song commercial that says: "everybody doesn't like something…" Well, I happen to not like a lot of things concerning boats and, in fact, I feel so strongly about some of these items that "don't like" turns to HATE. Now HATE is a strong word but it applies to everything I will talk about in this month's column.

I HATE it when I'm cruising in South Florida and "touch bottom" or, worse yet run aground in the <u>middle</u> <u>of</u> <u>the</u> <u>damn</u> <u>channel</u>! This always happens, when I am trying to impress influential clients or some scantily clad damsel. Give me northern cruising any day! Up there, channels are <u>channels</u> and not whispy little dredged ribbons that move about from day to day. In Long Island Sound, for example, you're either in deep water or on the rocks. No whimpy, limp wristed, moveable channels there! You either "is" or you "ain't" -- there's no in between.

I HATE people who bring matched sets of Gucci luggage aboard for a weekend stay. When this happens I make it a point to store them (the suitcases not the guests) in the bilge next to the dirtiest, smelliest, oiliest piece of equipment aboard.

I HATE guys who wear fake captain's hats with "scrambled eggs" on the visor. These are usually worn by guys that know zippo about boating, and, incidentally, they usually have scrambled eggs leftover from the morning's breakfast on their shirts too.

I HATE boat cushions that release air when sat upon, making you look like a disgusting slob. When this happens you usually flash an unconvincing grin and point meekly to the cushion. Of course, no one believes it was the cushion. I think this is the work of a small, perverted band of upholsterers who share their ideas and even fine tune their cushions for just the right sounds.

I HATE eating potato chips on teak decks. The chip residue falls onto the deck and the "30 weight" used motor oil they were fried in leaches into the wood and is almost impossible to remove. I've developed a method for eating potato chips (or any other oily food) on teak decks which is as follows: clamp your lips tightly around the chip while inhaling. Then break the chip off inside your mouth using your teeth. Remember, never stop inhaling. Every time you take a bite you inhale all the crumbs, salt, etc. This may seem like a strange way to ingest food and it may be funny to see a group of people, lips pursed around chips, making sucking noises on deck, and it may cause severe chocking if you inhale too hard, but it <u>does</u> keep the junk off the decks. If I had a boat with teak decks, I would post instructions for eating oily foods.

I HATE when I'm sleeping on a lower bunk and the guy over me, just back from a big night on the town, starts upchucking over the side of his berth. It's <u>not</u> funny! This happened to me on a cadet ship and is indelibly etched into my brain.

I HATE it when I have to squirm around in my car digging in my pockets for change at a toll booth. Inevitably any change I find falls between my legs into the seat. Then I stick my hand down there to root around for the change and invariably, I look up and there is a <u>bus</u> <u>full</u> of blue haired ladies on their way to a revival meeting looking down at me like I'm some kind of pervert. You may think this does not relate to boats, but since all my driving is boat related I am including it here.

I HATE lock tenders who ride bicycles.

I HATE inane conversations on VHF telephones:

"Yeah, this is the Sea Bunion calling Dog Drool, you there Harvey?"

"Yeah Oscar this is me, we're anchored over here at Bellybutton Cove, about to have a cookout."

Oscar: "Cookout? You use charcoal or wood?"

Harvey: "Well Oscar, I prefer charcoal but wood is okay too if you can get it."

Oscar: "Yeah wood is nice but charcoal is easy to get and they have this new stuff with the fluid built in so it lights real easy..."

I HATE boats that look like pregnant watermelons. This a result of stacking too many decks on too short a hull. Actually they shouldn't be called boats – they should be called "bloats".

I HATE meeting the Paddle Wheel Queen coming up (or down) the New River in Fort Lauderdale. This usually happens when rounding a blind curve in the river. The "Queen", though masterfully piloted, slows for nobody and is about as wide as the river.

I HATE it when I'm driving over a bridge and this fantastic, gold plated, one of a kind, never to be seen again power boat passes under and the damn bridge rail is always exactly in the right location to block the view.

I HATE boats painted red.

I HATE bright green pants with little sail boats printed all over them even more than bright red pants with little ship's wheels. Running a close third, is yellow pants with little square knots. This leads me to say that:

I HATE people who wear green pants with sail boats, red pants with ship's wheels or yellow pants with square knots which leads me to say that...

I HATE Lily Pulitzer and all she stands for.

Well, that gets all the HATE out of me for this month. Oh yeah... I HATE anyone who reads this column and doesn't like it.

October 1986

Pioneers of American Power Yachting

I am proud to say that my Family was at the forefront of the American power yachting movement.

I'm not talking about the ascot-clad pinky out for tea, arched eyebrow set who spoke in sing-song voices and gathered for cocktails on the fantail at 5:00. And I'm not speaking about palatial Victorian yachts with velvet settees, overstuffed leather chairs, bathtubs and wireless sets. And I'm not talking about vessels with names like "Corsair" or "Alva" or "Vanadis" or "North Star" which were powered by steam and looked like dismasted sailboats. If one were to compile a list of the great power yachtsmen of the world, names like John Jacob Astor, Cornelius Vanderbuilt, J. P. Morgan, Horace Dodge and Joseph Pulitzer would certainly be included. Nowhere on this list would the name Elias Fexas appear. And yet, Elias Fexas, my grandfather, his sons and others like him were the real pioneers of American power yachting. Mr. Astor, Mr. Vanderbuilt and their ilk were not power yachtsmen in the true sense of the word – with 50 man crew they were merely guests aboard their yachts. The traditionally accepted list of great American power yachtsmen should really be called "great American power yachts <u>visitors</u>". It was people like my grandfather who started the grassroots boating movement in the United States at the turn of the century setting out in long, narrow boats with one or two cylinder engines and no reverse gear. Before and immediately after World War I, these were the <u>real</u> power yachtsmen who put time in the trenches of early American power yachting and made power for every man what it is today.

Today we are boatsmen. These people were <u>BOATSMEN</u>! The modern day boatsman has it easy and, thinking about how it was in the beginning, makes one realize that we are really just nautical <u>wimps</u>. When was the last time you heard of a modern boatsman beaching his boat for repairs or caulking garboards or manually pumping bilges or hand cranking engines or even <u>rowing</u> for gosh sakes?

My grandfather immigrated to the United States from Greece in 1907. In the old country, he had been an engineer on freighters. Back then, the United States had an "open door" policy concerning immigration and he decided to settle in New York where, he was told, the streets were "paved with gold" (as it turned out, this was not far from the truth!). Not having enough money to bring his wife and children with him, he came (like so many others) alone, promising to send for his family as soon as he had the means to do so. He arrived in the midst of a worldwide depression, kicked off by the panic of 1907. His timing could not have been worse. There wasn't much work and, in desperation, he finally got a job as a bargeman. After three long years alone, he still hadn't accumulated enough money to send for his family. It was all over -- he would have to go back to Greece. One cold, New York winter evening, he was walking along a snowy street with his head down, depressed, when he saw something sparkling in the snow. He picked it up. It was a <u>diamond ring</u>! Stories about American streets being paved with gold <u>were</u> true! The ring (probably lost by one of the ascot and arched eyebrow set) allowed him to bring his family over (steerage class). If you saw it on "One Life to Live" you wouldn't believe it.

My grandfather started "yachting" as a business in 1908 with a 28' double ended converted steam launch with a full length wraparound glass cabin and single cylinder engine. Granddad began selling groceries to his former associates -- the bargemen who lived aboard anchored barges around Manhattan. This first boat was called "Chief" because that was the name she came with (to a newly arrive Greek immigrant, "Chief" must have sounded like a good American name). The family only made a few outings on this vessel before she was sold in 1910. A few years later he bought another boat which was used solely for pleasure. This second vessel was a 29' double ended, clinker built, converted lifeboat that had seen duty on deck of a ship before being turned into a "yacht". The price was $250 and she was named "Helas" (Helas means Greece). Buying a pleasure boat was a big move for a poor immigrant without much money and a large family to support -- which shows the commitment he had to boating. My grandmother (who was never crazy about boats anyhow) I am sure had her <u>own</u> ideas about how to spend $250 but, nevertheless, the boat was purchased. To accomplish this, my grandfather worked two jobs and most of his children also worked. My uncle, at the tender age of eight, worked two to three hours a day for a bookbinder and my father was a lamplighter.

"Helas" probably was the first (maybe the only) American pleasure yacht to be fired on by the American Navy. World War I started in 1917. Worried about the Germans attacking New York Harbor, the navy blockaded all entrances to the port. One summer's day "Helas" was steaming down the East River heading for Manhattan. My dad, then 13 years old, was at the helm, when, all of a sudden, two destroyers located off Whitestone started sounding sirens and whistles. "Helas" paid them no heed until they opened up on the little vessel straddling her with shells, bow and stern! Needless to say, this got everybody's attention and little "Helas" (which must have appeared to the navy to be a great threat to Manhattan) was promptly brought to a stop. When brought alongside the ship, they were informed that, had "Helas" not stopped, the third round was aimed <u>between</u> the first two! As it turned out, rules were in effect stating that all vessels entering New York Harbor had to stop and identify themselves. Waterway guides not being prevalent at the time, the crew on "Helas" never got the word.

"Helas" originally had a small cabin forward with the engine installed aft, out in the open. Having a big family (wife, 3 daughters and 3 sons) Granddad wanted more cabin space so (with what must have been considerably effort and expense) he moved the engine forward and built a larger forward cabin while adding a new aft cabin. When the boat was launched after the conversion, the propeller was half out of the water! This may give our family claim to having invented the first surface piercing propeller, but I'm not sure. The drill was that whenever the boat was to get underway, guests and family were asked to move to the stern!

"Helas" leaked such that merely keeping her afloat was a major accomplishment. In fact, "Helas" leaked <u>so</u> badly she would be anchored off the beach so that, at low tide, she would be "high and dry", at which time someone went down and opened a seacock to drain the bilge (the first automatic bilge pump?).

In the summer of 1918, the whole family moved from their tenement in lower Manhattan aboard the "Helas" in an effort to escape and infantile paralysis (polio) epidemic. The season was spent at North Beach (an amusement park which is now LaGuardia Airport), a popular anchorage back then. There was a boatyard there called Rays and the area was easily accessible by trolley car. As it turned out, a number of children in the tenement where the family lived did come down with polio.

One stormy night in 1919 the anchor gave way and the boat was wrecked, putting my grandfather out of his misery. Grandad was not long without a boat or misery. He soon bought another in 1920 which he called "Mary F" after one of his daughters. This boat was much roomier with a "wide beam" of 8' and a length of 36'. Back then there were no such things as "stock" or production line boats. Boats were either built by a professional yard on a custom basis or designed and fabricated by amateurs builders. "Mary F" was just such a vessel, being designed and built by a <u>trombone player</u>, off all things! This fellow drew on what he knew best -- music and, since he couldn't very well pattern the boat after a trombone, he copied the shape of a mandolin. She had very round bilges and the planks at the stern were brought together in a rounded configuration ending in a tiny transom just like a mandolin. With her minimal beam and very round underbody she rolled terribly. Nevertheless, she remained in the family for 21 years, consuming three engines.

What was boating like for the average man during these early days? To give you an idea of "yachting" back then, I quote my father who was seen it all from the inception of power boating to today's rocket ship boats: "There were no stock boats in those days and the times were not affluent for the working classes. The result was that many built their own boats that were a travesty to the art of boat designing. Others did better by converting sailboats to motorboats. The average speed was about 7 mph and boats did not travel too far from their home base. One had to be hearty to own a boat. You had to be a mechanic, carpenter, caulker, painter and plumber to keep your boat up as few people could afford to hire professional services. And you had to have strong muscles to bail out the boat (as most leaked) and to row the dinghy (there were no outboards at that time) and to start the motor. The motors of the day were one or two cylinders affair and balky in starting. Many of the two cycle engines had no reverse gear. If you wanted to reverse you turned off the ignition switch until the motor reached its last revolution and started to "kick back". Then you would put on the switch and the engine would turn backwards! That gave you a great reverse but if the trick did not work, you had to use your carpentry skills afterward!"

In those days, simply <u>starting</u> an engine was a big deal. This, of course, is taken from granted today. Again, quoting my dad: "there was no generator or starter and you had to use muscles to turn the heavy flywheel with a crank or lever to start the motor. If it backfired, you either hurt your arms or were hurled around by the lever. We would go out to the boat A COUPLE OF HOURS (!!!) before the guests arrived to start the engine. It required a lot of turning, but once started and warmed up, it would start again without difficulty. The oiling system consisted of a glass oil gage that dripped oil into the cylinders. Bearings below were oiled by a splash system. Needless to say, a lot of oil splashed around and the "yachtsmen" wore coveralls and kept a bunch of waste (wadded cotton strings) in his back pocket to wipe things up".

The "Mary F"! I've heard stories about this boat all my life. Talk about leaky boats! The "Mary F" would half sink every three days. If she had been left longer than that, the water would have been raised above the toilet and she would have completely sunk. To say she had limber garboard planks would be an understatement. Every spring, the garboard seams (perhaps "gaps" would be a better term) were packed with caulking and covered with a molding embedded in putty. All this only served to keep her afloat about three days. One day a small fish (we used to call them "killies") was found swimming in the bilge. It had made its way up through the garboard seam! My uncle Mike tells the story of going to the boat Wednesday evenings with a date for a cruise. After working at the manual bilge pump for over an hour he would then pump the water out of the engine and change the oil (since the crankcase went under). After all this, he was still faced with the monumental task of hand cranking the engine to get it started. He did this nearly <u>every</u> Wednesday. She must have been quite a date!

Then there was the smokestack story. From the turn of the century through the 1920's almost every respectable powerboat whether steam powered or not <u>had</u> to have a smokestack -- an influence of the great steamships of the day. Smokestacks were a status symbol like satellite communications domes are today. They gave a boat class. They made a boat look like a "little ship". Back then, immigrants coming to the United States would choose a ship with the most smokestacks since they thought they indicated speed, power and prestige. Four pipe steamships were common. Little did the immigrants know that, back then, steamship companies were installing "dummy" stacks merely to impress the travelers. Anyway, one day it was decided that "Mary F" needed a "smokestack" even though she was powered by a gasoline engine with an exhaust out the stern. Not only did she need a smokestack but she needed a <u>whistle</u> mounted on it. The stack was fabricated by a friend of my grandfather who worked at a metal shop in downtown Manhattan and my dad had the task of transporting it by trolley to North Beach. When the motorman saw this young fellow trying to drag a big smokestack on the trolley he wouldn't let him aboard, but some fast talking persuaded him and the smokestack was taken to the boat for installation on the trunk cabin. The fact that it greatly obstructed vision from the helm just aft was of no consequence. There were "cable" standoffs required to support the structure. The "steam whistle" was, in reality, powered by a small air pump driven off the main engine. Then there is the apparel. I am told it was common to dress this way -- straw hats, bow ties, blazers and all – when <u>going to</u> and <u>returning from</u> the boat. This, of course, was all a sham since, once aboard, the uniform of the day would be dirty coveralls or bathing suits.

Yes, the Mary F was responsible for most of the family's boating legends like the spaghetti incident -- a great example of Murphy's Law. "Mary F" was running from Glenn Cove (a popular weekend retreat) across Long Island Sound to New Rochelle, her home port. A strong northeast wind was driving huge waves down the Sound and "Mary F", with her mandolin bottom, was rolling terribly -- so much so that a "zig zag" course was steered to avoid beam seas. Somewhere midtrip, someone decided to heat a pot of spaghetti sauce for dinner upon arrival. It is important to note that, back then, one lived intimately with one's engine. Engines weren't buried below -- it was common for the engine to be installed in the middle of the cabin with a table top over it and all sides exposed. This was the case on "Mary F". Inevitably the pot of spaghetti slid off the stove making a mess of the cabin. My uncle broke out the mop and started cleaning, but the vessel was lurching so badly that, somehow, the mop caught in the open engine, stopping it. Then the boat really started rolling. Things got so bad that life jackets were broken out, but the engine was soon started and "Mary F" eventually made landfall, less one spaghetti dinner.

Then there was the stern anchoring incident. This story came about when landlubber guests were aboard. It was common back then to drop an anchor off the stern and run the bow of the boat close to shore for swimming, picnicking, etc. On this particular day, one of the landlubber guests was put in charge of the stern anchor. He was assured that there was nothing to it: when given the signal he would simply drop the anchor over the stern and pay out line. No problem. When the signal was given the anchor was dropped over the stern and the guest started paying out line... and paying out line... and paying out more line. Suddenly, he came to the bitter end. Panic! What to do? Well, it was obvious to him what to do. Grasping the bitter end of the line in his hand he dutifully jumped off the stern so as not to lose the anchor!

The impression I get from all the stories I have heard was that life on the "Mary F" was one big Marx Brothers movie and, in fact, the family home movies taken aboard enforce this impression. "Mary F" provided a summer home afloat for the family from 1920 to 1941 -- the beginning of World War II -- when she was abandoned at a boatyard. The United States was going to war and there would be little time (or gasoline) for boats.

The "Chief", "Helas" and "Mary F" were predecessors of many family boats to come. My dad bought a nearly new 32'

Wheeler in 1943 (only to have her wrecked by the great hurricane of '44). He bought another Wheeler in 1947 (which was the boat I grew up on during 20 summers) followed by two Elcos. After the war, uncle Mike bought and old commuter boat which was followed by another Wheeler (Wheelers were big back then) and then a Chris Craft. My uncle John had a Richardson. My cousin Dean who grew up on the "Mary F" had had six boats -- mostly Chris Crafts. In all, I count 17 family boats after "Mary F". After the war, four family boats were moored at Northport on Long Island and cruised together for about 20 years. Two of them remain there to this day and 76 years after starting on "Helas", my dad and his brothers are <u>still</u> boating together.

It is hard to believe that, were it not for a diamond ring found in the snow one cold night in Manhattan, none of this would have happened. I certainly wouldn't be writing this now. Were it not for that ring, I probably would be a goat roper on the Island of Smyrna in the Mediterranean. Or, if I was lucky, I might have been designing caiques -- gaily painted, double ended boats used by fisherman in the Mediterranean. Only in America.

November 1986

A Plea For Low Tech

It is 1992. You are in the Gulfstream making a run from Ft. Lauderdale to Bimini at your customary 50 knot cruising speed in your brand new Berteras (when boats became too expensive and complicated to build due to "high tech", small boat companies fell by the wayside and larger ones found it necessary to pool their resources). The computer controlled digital instrument panels in front of you blink blue liquid crystallized facts and figures at you. The central computer on board controls fuel management, steering and throttle setting while monitoring engine functions, pumping bilges and making you coffee in the morning. Your fiberglass and ceramic diesel engines are smoothly purring beneath the deck when, suddenly, the information panel at the helm station goes blank and the engines die as your Berteras slides off plane and starts wallowing in the nasty eight foot (and building) seas of the Gulfstream.

Being in boating all your life, you pride yourself on being self-sufficient at sea so you grab your tool box and open the engine room door to see what's happened. You pop a trouble shooting program into the engine room computer and crank the engines. The computer impassively informs you that the fuel management circuit is malfunctioning. Meanwhile the seas are growing vicious and the boat is lurching violently without the assist of her computer controlled stabilizers. On the inboard side of the engine lies a huge black box. You unlatch the cover, lift it off its gasket and look inside. What you see is a jungle of printed circuits, diodes and computer chips. You stand there dejected with your crescent wrench in one hand and a screwdriver in the other as you realize that there is no way in hell you are ever going to fix these engines without a masters degree in electronics. You get on the telephone and call the Drug Enforcement Agency Coastal Patrol for a tow (the DEA took over the Coast Guard in 1990 when they realized the Coast Guard was expending 95% of their manpower preventing drugs from entering the States).

This little scenario is not nearly as silly as it might sound. A while back, I wrote an article about how the marine industry trails the automotive industry in styling by about five years. As I promised, the "blob" look from the automotive industry is creeping into the marine field and more floating blobs are appearing every year (there will be more on this topic in the future). What I <u>didn't</u> say in that piece is that, not only does the marine industry trail the automotive industry in <u>styling</u> by five years, but also in <u>mechanicals/electronics</u>. This is a truly scary, pervasive trend.

I have always advocated "high tech" marine construction:

lightweight, aluminum and composite construction using exotic foams, carbon fiber, Kevlar, unidirectional, biaxial, triaxial reinforcements and exotic, high strength resins. Yacht construction deals with structure -- you can look at something and either it's broke or it ain't -- no two ways about it. Similarly, marine engines and systems have traditionally been mechanical in nature. You could look at something and see how it worked or if it was malfunctioning. A broken chain link on a mechanical steering system, a leaking hydraulic line, a sheared bolt, a bent valve, no spark from the coil or distributor, a ruptured fuel pump diaphragm, etc., are all things you can study and understand how they function (or malfunction) and troubleshoot. Till now, a guy with basic mechanical knowledge could go down in the bilge with a set of tools and fix a problem himself.

But look what is happening! Marine engine manufacturers are introducing fuel injection to their gasoline engines and breakerless ignitions and computerized engine controls. The latest fuel injection systems are of the "port injection" type where a computer sends a command to a little solenoid valve at each cylinder telling it when to open and close. This type of system can't be far behind on diesel engines either. Scary! Some larger yachts are already controlled by "fly by wire" systems where steering and engine controls are cycled purely through electric impulses via wires. More scary! In a hydraulic system, you can look at lines and cylinders to detect a malfunction but you can't "see" and electric leak. You can't look at a printed circuit board and see if there is a problem. You can't "see" what's going on inside those funny little diodes and chips.

I have the pleasure of owning two Corvettes. One is a 1971 coupe powered by a monster 454 engine. The other is Corvette's latest, greatest, high tech effort. The old car is nice and I feel at home with it. Since I bought it new, I have personally done virtually all the mechanical work needed. It's got a big four barrel Rochester carburetor. Your foot is directly connected to the rotors at each corner of the car via hydro-mechanical brakes. It's got analog instrumentation. The HVAC system is controlled by push/pull cables and vacuum servos. It's a great, powerful and dependable car and, with my little tool box that I carry around with me, I feel confident that I can repair nearly any malfunction that might occur on the road and get myself home. The new 'Vette is great too, but it scares me. It's got ABS brakes (a computer brain is inserted between your foot and the brake pads). It's got an incomprehensible electronic ignition system containing electronic "boards" with acronym names like "PROM". It's got an automatic electronic "climate control system". If the old 'Vette dies, I can go out with my wrenches and screwdrivers and a big hammer and usually fix the damn thing quickly. When my new Corvette dies, well... when I got the car I permanently engraved on my driver's license the number of a <u>towing company</u>! And you know what's coming down the line? Computer controlled <u>suspension systems</u> will replace springs and shocks. Rear wheels will steer in tandem with the fronts. Steering and throttle functions will be electronically controlled. Distributorless ignitions will be the norm. Pretty soon you won't even be able to <u>tow</u> the sombitch away unless the computer is operational. The question is: "is my gewgaw and computer chip laden new Corvette better than the old one?" The answer is: "maybe when it it's running". But the first time that it lets me down on the Florida Turnpike at 2:00 a.m. in the rain or when the "7" in my beautiful $2500 liquid crystal instrument pod turns to a "1" then ask me which is the better car. The thing is, when you crap out on the road, it's usually not a life threatening situation (unless you live in South Florida where it's not the elements but the local element that's dangerous). Mechanical failure at sea can be very dangerous: your dead vessel could be bashed on the rocks or rammed or hit by lightning or pooped by a huge sea. Give me low tech at sea! Give me systems I can look at and understand. Give me good stuff that moves up and down, opens and closes and rotates and slides and twists! Give me electrical systems I can check by grounding a screwdriver on the block and watching the little spark jump (watching sparks jump is a very satisfying experience somehow). The way cars are now and the way boats soon will be, you would no sooner attempt to fix your marine engine than you would attempt to fix your IBM PC! I was brought up on a power boat and in my 44 years of boating with my family and alone, I can only remember having a mechanic aboard maybe twice -- not because we couldn't fix the problem, but because our trouble shooting was flawed. Today, musclebound, tattooed mechanics are being replaced by pale, skinny computer nerd with tape on their glasses. "Shadetree mechanics" will soon be a thing of the past. In fact, mechanics are already a dying breed. What we have now are <u>parts</u> <u>changers</u> with nerd names like "Mr. Goodwrench"! No longer are problems "trouble shot" but, rather, parts and electrical boards are swapped at random until the problem is corrected.

You're probably saying "if it was up to this guy, radios and televisions would still have huge vacuum tubes and a "desk top" computer would fill up an entire room". Not so. High tech is fine on non-vital systems. And don't tell me about 747's and the space shuttle that rely on electronics. Sure they do, but these systems have <u>full</u> <u>time</u> <u>engineers</u> attending them and have backups on their backups on their backups -- sometimes as many as <u>five</u> redundant systems. High tech vital ships systems have no business at sea unless a full time "Goodwrench" is carried aboard.

Like, I've said, it's really scary and, pretty soon, you and I will be as helpless at sea as I am in my new car when a failure takes place. If you want a good, long term investment buy a TOWBOAT STOCK now because, soon, the waters will be littered with helpless, drifting boats. There was a time when I looked down on poor, helpless, hapless people who couldn't fix things themselves. Now, <u>I'm</u> becoming one of them and I don't like it. It's a sad situation... Think I'll take my '71 'Vette out for a drive.

December 1986

Where The Boats Are

Fort Lauderdale, Florida. What can you say about a place that has <u>topless</u> <u>donut</u> <u>shops</u>? "Would you like some milk for your coffee?" a lovely naked waitress said to me as I sat there, java in hand, not knowing where to look, "Yes", I said, pondering the possibilities as she whipped out her milk pitcher from under the counter. Fort Lauderdale... Where the boys are. Where the girls are. Where the <u>boats</u> are. Glitz town, U.S.A. A town where the majority of Mercedes cars are AMG conversions. A town where the daylight hookers along Federal Highway can't be told from the "good girls" walking the same street without a score card because they all dress alike. Fort Lauderdale...Boat nut's paradise with more large yachts per square mile than anywhere else in the world. A city of a thousand boat yards... A city where 120 footers are rafted up in marinas side-by-side like so many 21 foot inboard/outboards... A city that hosts the world's largest floating boat show.

The Fort Lauderdale Boat Show, held at the end of October, is, indeed, the world's largest in-the-water boat show. It's also the most crowded and confusing boat show on the face of the earth. Can it be that only eight years ago (when I attended my first Lauderdale show) it occupied only the south side of Bahia Mar and essentially used the existing concrete docks with little else added? Nowadays, it's hard to remember this is a <u>floating</u> boat show because you don't see much water. About every square inch of water surface is covered by fiberglass, aluminum, steel or wood. The show is <u>so</u> confusing it's hard to understand how anyone shopping for a boat could attend this show and make a rational decision. The reason why the boat show got this way is simple: GREED. It's a nasty word folks, but it's true. Simply <u>greed</u> by both the boat show organizers and the exhibitors make this show what it is (or isn't). Boats of every description, size and type are crammed in cheek-to-jowl, nose-to-tail (some bows overlapping sterns), covering every available area of water. This not only occurs on the south side of the marina but, as of last year, the plague has spread to the north side also. Next year, I hear the show will occupy the <u>entire</u> <u>intercostal waterway</u> from Bahia Mar to Pier 66, but this is only a rumor.

If you're in the boat business, a phrase you'll hear over and over is "nobody buys boats at the boat shows". Generally, this is true and I think I know why. I'd always thought that the way a product was <u>presented</u> was at least as important as the product itself. It's the old steak and sizzle game. At Lauderdale they are selling only ground beef... nary a sizzle to be found anywhere. The scene now shifts to Bloomingdales in Manhattan (stay with me folks, there is a point to all this). Bloomingdales and other stores like it spend great amounts of time and money on their window displays. If they are displaying clothes they are hung on slender, angular (slangular?) mannequins frozen in all sort of strange positions to catch the eye. If it's a fall display, dried leaves swirled by hidden fans might surround the mannequin's feet. Friends of the first mannequin occupy the rest of the window wearing different outfits. Other articles of clothing might be strategically draped on a fence post or displayed on a bush. The window backdrop might be a scene from New England in the fall with a Cape Cod house and picked fences. A cocker spaniel is running to the door with a newspaper in his mouth. If you stand at the window and look hard enough you can picture <u>yourself</u> there wearing those clothes. Although you are 4'10" and 280 pounds, you are also "slangular". Such is the allure of artfully displayed products. Now picture the same window with a plain pipe rack running from side to side upon which are hung hangers -- cheap, skinny wire hangers, the kind without the cardboard tubes on them -- jammed against one another containing the same clothes the mannequins wore. Not a very alluring display, eh? Or how about a jewelry store which normally displays its goods on soft velvet pads in lit glass cases. Imagine what the effect would be with a pile of rings, necklaces and earrings displayed in a cardboard box? Would you buy a car from a showroom that was grid locked like an Italian intersection at rush hour? The same applies to boat shows and, as far as Fort Lauderdale is concerned, it's plain pipe rack and hanger time. With the majority of the boats displayed "stern to" the docks, it's like trying to evaluate a flower held stem side up or a painting with the frame on edge or a woman with her back to you. From the stern the simple fact is that most boats look alike and, if the truth be told, the stern-on view is most unbecoming -- all you see are doors and exhaust pipes. What does this have to do with <u>greed</u>? Well, greedy exhibitors who paid a lot of money to rent water space try to wedge every available boat into the space they have paid for on the theory that: "more is better"... "something for everybody"..."dazzle 'em with numbers". The show promoters are equally at fault by allowing this craziness to take place. Hell, even <u>car salesman</u> in checkered suits and alligator shoes know better. At car shows, new cars are commonly shown in elaborate displays with carpeted or marble floors, or on turntables. There is music in the background and the cars are displayed at different angles with enough space between them to be admired. Lights dance off sparkling paint work and beautiful, scantily clad models roam about.

A walk through the Fort Lauderdale Boat Show reminds one of a gigantic Turkish bazaar or the famous floating villages of Hong Kong. Things are not completely hopeless though and, as usual, I have some suggestions that will probably upset some people.

Suggestion #1: Get the damn broker boats out of the show. They don't belong there and simply confuse things. Fall boat shows are intended to display boat lines for the new season. You won't find used cars displayed side-by-side with new models in car shows or even car show rooms. No, they are banished to the "used car lot" (which is, incidentally, usually completely separate from the new car lot). Give the broker boats a separate area if necessary (how about a concurrent broker boat show at Pier 66?), but move them out!

Suggestion #2: Group similar types of vessels together when possible. Seen in Lauderdale were rows of various and sundry boats jammed together. One row included large yachts, tiny cruisers, large sailboats, trawlers, sportfishermen, and superboats, without rhyme or reason.

Suggestion #3: Eliminate duplication. Many new boat companies had duplicate models at the show. Example: two Ocean 63's docked stern to stern along the outer pier. For what? Because one had a pink mouton interior while the other was done in red velvet? Come on guys! There must have been a dozen Hatteras 58' motor yachts at the show. For what? Here again, most of the problem is broker boats.

Suggestion #4: Spread out the displays so one can see what one is buying. The reason "nobody buys boats at the boat shows" is because people can't see the damn thing.

Display is everything! Back in 1978 when the Midnight Lace was introduced at Fort Lauderdale Boat Show an important reason she was so highly acclaimed, I believe, was the way she was displayed. In '78 things were not so crowded and frantic and the prototype 44' Lace was assigned a slot alongside one of the few floating docks. At the time, only the concrete docks were used for display allowing much space between the rows of boats. An anchor was set to the west (try doing that now guys!) holding the vessel approximately 10 feet off the float and parallel to it. A bridge was constructed for boarding and flood lights were installed under the dock to light the boat from water level at night.

This simple display was <u>so</u> effective that crowds gathered on the float standing there observing the boat in her entirety in profile from a distance. So large were the crowds that, at times, the floats were submerged! Had this first Lace been crammed in "stern to" among other boats, I'm certain the Midnight Lace line would not exist today.

Amongst exhibitors with multiple boats at the '86 show, Bertram stood out as being smart enough not to load all their available water space with boats. Empty slips were allotted between boats so that each could be viewed at a distance and admired. Not coincidentally, Bertram sold a good number of boats at the show this year. COME ON EXHIBITORS, WISE UP! THIS AIN'T NO TURKISH BAZAAR. THIS AIN'T NO USED CAR LOT IN NEW JOISY. THIS IS A <u>BOAT</u> <u>SHOW</u>. People come because they <u>love</u> and <u>appreciate</u> boats, but they can't appreciate what they can't see! I have some good ideas about how boats should be presented at boat shows. Boat exhibits should have <u>themes</u> and a few bucks spent on props and backgrounds will pay off handsomely. I can see it all now...

THE CRUISING THEME: A large cruiser is <u>anchored</u> (not tied to the dock) diagonally in the area occupying two slips (the stern is kept from swinging by a hidden anchor attached to the running gear). The entire underwater area of the display is separated from the marina water by a huge, submerged canvas bag extending slightly above the surface. Using dye, the water within this enclosure is tinted bright aqua. The backdrop is a huge canvas of the South Sea Islands. Palm trees lining the docks sway in breeze. Exotic birds are perched about. The exhibit is stocked with porpoises that periodically breach the surface in pairs. Tahitian music plays in the background along with native drums. Divers emerge from the depths with fresh lobster to be cooked on board. Flaxen haired nymphettes frolic about in the water. Lit from below at night, the water casts a glow over everything. The display is covered by a huge light blue nylon cover simulating the sky. Fat, pink clouds would be glued to the underside of this "sky". Wow! What an exhibit! How could anybody resist this? WHERE DO I SIGN? I WANT TO GO CRUISING!

THE SPORTFISHING THEME: Here a larger space has been taken -- a total of four slips -- two opposite each other and the area between them. The area is isolated by a wide mesh underwater fence. A big brooding sportfisherman is maneuvering in this closed space with growling engines. An electric wavemaker produces rollers that rock the boat. The captain is on the bridge, the mate is in the cockpit and the owner is in the fighting chair as the theme from "Victory at Sea" plays on the boat stereo. Suddenly on cue, a <u>trained thousand pound blue marlin</u> strikes the bait and the fight is on. WHAT A SHOW! People clap and cheer as the boat furiously maneuvers in the tight space and the angler fights the fish (which has been taught to leap every 15 seconds). Buyers are six deep around the exhibit waving their checkbooks in a buying frenzy. What a great show! TAKE MY CHECK!

THE "DOCKSIDE ANGLER" THEME: Here the backdrop would be a posh waterfront hotel. Tied in front of it would be a sleek, offshore runabout about 50' long with eight engines and a 37 color paint job. A suntanned, potbellied man in a bikini, obviously the owner, laden with gold necklaces, three gold wristwatches and four diamond rings sits in the cockpit. The hair on his chest is supplemented by a chest toupee. Suddenly a beautiful bikini-clad woman walks by. Before you know it, she is aboard the boat and <u>disappears</u> <u>below</u> <u>decks</u> <u>with</u> <u>the</u> <u>owner</u>! Background music swells. They emerge in slightly disarray 20 minutes later. The crowd gasps! The owner takes the "trolling seat" in the cockpit again. A few minutes later <u>two</u> women walk by and before you know what is happening <u>they</u> disappear below with the owner. WHAT A GREAT BOAT THIS MUST BE! Policemen surround the exhibit with locked arms to hold back the crowds who are forcing blank checks upon the salesmen. THIS IS GREAT!

Yes, this could happen to you, exhibitors, if only a little imagination is used. DISPLAY IS EVERYTHING! The atmosphere at the Fort Lauderdale show, as it presently exist is too crowded, too confusing and too harrying to sell boats. I will say, however, that the Fort Lauderdale Boat Show is superbly managed and if this managerial talent is applied to making the boat something special, all involved will benefit. Showmanship is what made America great. Bring on the nymphettes! Cue the trained marlin!

January 1987

The Blobs Are Coming!

This is <u>not</u> the name of a bad Japanese monster movie featuring creatures that look like melted marshmallows with faces and make "Gumpa, Gumpa, Gumpa" noises like a toilet plunger when they move. The blobs I'm referring to are <u>real</u> and pervasive. They will be encountered by everyone on this planet in their daily lives and, if we're not careful, they will engulf and consume us all.

God, I love to gloat! Gloating is one of the best feelings in the world. There at the end of the big boat hall at the '86 Genoa Boat Show stood "Kineo", a metallic gray projectile of a sportboat designed by Ferry Porsche for the Italian boat market. To say the styling was rounded in nature would be an understatement -- the boat looked like warm syrup poured on mounds of ice cream. The entire superstructure appeared to be oozing. When I first saw the boat I labeled it a "giant recumbent lady in shrink wrap" for that is exactly what it looked like. In April 1985 I wrote a piece called "Yachting Styling: The Squares vs The Rounds" expressing my surprise that Italian yacht stylists had belatedly rediscovered curves.

Now I <u>like</u> curves. Curves are sensuous, warm and friendly and I use them liberally in my designs. Until two or three years ago though, most Italian boats looked like origami -- folded paper objects the Japanese consider art. Originally conceived during the '50's and '60's to produce modern looking structures out of sheet plywood, the sharply creased Italian styling was, at the time, <u>functional</u>. When fiberglass came to the fore, the Italians unbelievably continued utilizing razor styling for <u>twenty years</u>, although fiberglass can be molded to virtually any shape whatsoever. This aberration continued until about two years ago when I started noticing curves creeping into Italian yacht styling. That's when I wrote the story and ended that piece with the following mildly prophetic statement: "If I know the Italians, they will carry their newly discovered roundness to the extreme and, soon, the boats will look like crayolas left out in the sun too long or, perhaps, a well-used candle. After this happens, you can rest assured that sharp creases will be back again." Well, it's happening folks. Italians indeed are using curves big time. Gloat. Gloat. Boy I love it when I'm right! I am <u>surprised</u>, however, that it happened so rapidly.

Yes, the rounded look in boats is officially <u>in</u>, being sanctioned by the traditional world styling leaders, the Italians, and the era of "CREEPING BLOBISM" is quickly approaching. In this case, however, the Italians didn't start the trend -- it was started right here in America when companies like Trojan took the first bold step away from the creased look. The Italians are now embracing the concept and, indeed, already carrying it to the excess. It won't be long before most Italians yachts will become blobs looking like giant waterlogged kapok life jackets cast adrift or floating walruses.

Blame it on the auto industry which, as I have said before, leads the yacht industry by about five years when it comes to styling. The auto industry worldwide is now churning out very round production cars and show cars resembling big jellyfish. It is literally impossible to tell the front from the back on some of these creations without looking to see where the damn steering wheel is! Chevrolet, Buick and Oldsmobile are among the worst offenders. The Chevy Corvette, Buick Wildcat and Oldsmobile Aerotech are all rolling blobs having a distinct lack of personality and all looking essentially alike. Think you have trouble finding your car in a crowded parking lot now? When the blob look is in full vogue, parking lots will look like racks full of cream puffs at the bakery. When you get into extreme blobism, auto and yacht designers have a problem: there are only a certain number of ways you can <u>style</u> a blob. Let's face it, a <u>blob</u> is a <u>blob</u> -- be it an amoeba, a blob of whipped cream, tar, automobile or yacht. How can you differentiate between one amoeba and another -- you can't. They all look alike. They have no character. They are nondescript. Hell, even <u>amoebas</u> can't tell one amoeba from the other. Guy amoebas can't identify girl amoebas so they have to reproduce <u>themselves</u> by splitting in two, which doesn't sound like much fun. Think of it! No candlelight, no wine, no soft music, no cigarrete afterwards. Just divide yourself in two and continue about your business.

The triple engined, 80 knot Porsche designed speedboat

described at the opening of this article is a portent of things to come. The foredeck of this vessel looks like the hood of the Porsche 911 -- while undoubtedly beautiful, it is completely nonfunctional. Forward of the cockpit is no man's land. There are no walkways, no handrails, no toe rails, and no nonskid areas anywhere. If the dictum that "form follows function" is true, then the function of this design must be to provide the world's fastest mobile waterslide. You can't even grab a cleat on the way over the side -- they are hidden beneath faired in covers. If you buy this boat, a pair of <u>spiderman shoes</u> should be standard equipment. Observing the boat from the balcony one thought kept crossing my mind: "How many Italian yuppies will slide over the side of this boat in the name of <u>high style</u>? And what will they be thinking on the way down?

As always, there are some reactionaries. One yacht stylist of note is currently into grafting '57 Plymouth tailfins onto large motor yachts to create a ... well, "unique" look. While a '57 Plymouth indeed is a unique looking car, it never won any design awards and tailfin-bedecked cars are now considered "camp", just as gaudy jukeboxes are. Tailfins were a nonfunctional styling aberration on cars and it is my personal feeling that the same applies to boats. You won't find a super-successful entrepreneur driving a '57 Plymouth with its garish tailfins, ginza-strip tail lights, man-eater front end and spinner hub caps. No, he'd be driving something more elegant, like a Rolls Royce or Mercedes. I personally cannot fathom why some of these same people are opting for tailfins on their megayachts.

Italian interiors are also approaching blobism. The

"padded cell" look is currently in vogue and rounded corners are seen on joinerwork everywhere, although, again, in most cases this is <u>nonfunctional</u>. Let's talk about fiddles. Fiddles are raised rails around flat surfaces like tabletops, countertops and cabinet tops for the purpose of preventing objects from sliding off when the boat rolls. They have traditionally been fitted to all boats until recently. Fiddles are now "<u>out</u>" on European (and many American boats) but after a couple of plates of marinara-laden spaghetti go careening off the dining table onto the $500 per square yard custom woven, one-of-a-kind carpet depicting scenes from the Sistine Chapel or numerous goblets of burgundy have slid off the beautifully rounded bar tops onto the snow white carpeting, I imagine that fiddles will fast make a comeback.

Other styling trends were noted at the Genoa Boat Show. The infamous exhaust blisters pioneered by the Italians (exhaust is routed from the engineroom <u>outside</u> the hull and covered by a fiberglass or aluminum housing (projecting 12" or 16" out from the topsides) is fast losing favor after most of these beauties have been cleaned off, or at least damaged, during Italian docking maneuvers. There is a rumor these exhaust fairings were invented by greedy owners of Italian boatyards looking for a fast way to increase their repair revenues, but this cannot be substantiated. In any case, only a few external exhaust cowlings were noted at the show -- the majority of exhausts now reposes conventionally at the transom or lead underwater, where they really belong.

Other trends: transoms are starting to rake forward, asymmetrical radar arches which are essentially only half an arch (this will take some getting used to folks) are gaining popularity and oval portholes are virtually standard equipment on all Italian boats. Hidden, mechanized gangways and metallic paint jobs are also gaining in popularity.

Ironically, it is the Italians that may eventually lead us away from blobism. When the Ferrarri Testarossa was introduced two years ago, Ferrari eschewed the blob look. After experiments, I am sure, with blob shapes the styling studio of Pininfarina decided to adopt the "jet fighter plane philosophy". Although considerable work was done in the wind tunnel a <u>new</u> <u>functionalism</u> blending the aero look with interesting styling features (giving the car <u>character</u>) seems to have emerged with the Testarossa, which hopefully will catch on and produce a new crop of distinctively styled automobiles... and yachts.

In the meantime, RUN FOR YOUR LIVES THE BLOBS ARE COMING (GUMPA, GUMPA, GUMPA). If one comes into your marina or you see one approaching in your rear view mirror, get away <u>fast</u> or it might engulf you in a cocoon of sameness. One more thing. The next time you have a "sure thing" hot date, take time for a moment of silence on behalf of poor amoebas everywhere.

February 1987

Don't Put Down The New York Boat Show (or It's Hot Dogs)

New York City, New York: New York City unquestionably has the finest mechanics/body and fender men in the world. Forget the Ferrari Formula One Team. Forget Roger Penske's Indy pit crew and forget the Porsche racing team. Mechanics and body men in New York City have them <u>all</u> beat.

Working with primitive, basic tools under less than ideal working conditions, these guys perform true miracles providing unmatched speedy, low costs service. Example: driving from Long Island to New York for the 77th Annual New York Boat Show I observed alongside the Grand Central Parkway two cars that had just been involved in a crackup. These were newer, late model cars, one a Chevy and one a Datsun, I believe. On the way back from the show that same day, approximately four hours later, the same two cars were still there but they were transformed -- mere shadows of their former magnificence. Yes, they had been <u>picked</u> <u>clean</u> by the famous vulture mechanics/body and fender men of New York City. I MEAN PICKED CLEAN! I'm talking about major mechanical operations here. How in the hell do you remove a car engine at the side of a major New York highway without lift equipment and do it fast enough so as not to attract the wrath of New York's finest? The engines were gone, all the glass was gone (ever try to remove a windshield?), the hood and trunk lids were gone, fenders were gone, wheels, axles, bumpers. EVERYTHING! Left only were carcasses! No doubt about it, when I have major mechanical or body/fender work to be done on any of my cars I am taking them to New York!

I was in the Big Apple for the Christmas/New Year holiday and to catch the new New York Boat Show at the Jacob K. Javits Convention Center. Now the New York Boat Show has, of late, not been the greatest of boat shows. Boating people "in the know" tended to look down their noses at the New York show and, admittedly, after shows the likes of Genoa, Italy, Fort Lauderdale and Miami, the New York Show looked rather shabby -- to be forever relegated to inboard/outboard boats for the rest of its existence. But don't count New York out as a major boat show exhibition center. In the past, we may have looked at the New York Show with scorn but remember that New York City is where the boat business, as we know it today started. Think about it! A boat show in 1910 must have been a pretty radical thing and the first boat show was held in little ol' New York. A while later in the '20's when there were no friendly neighborhood boat dealers to buy boats from, progressive boat manufacturers opened up showrooms along Park and Fifth Avenues in Manhattan to display and sell their products. A good example is the famous "Port Elco" salon in New York. Elco built the first production powerboats and initially sold them through these outlets. The boat business owes much to New York. During the last few years, however, the boat show, held at the old New York Coliseum, was losing its luster year by year. The boats got smaller, the displays sparser, and the hot dogs soggier. I personally hadn't attended a New York Boat Show for a few years however, but I wanted to be at this one for a couple of reasons.

First, it was being held in a magnificent new building -- the Jacob K. Javits Convention Center on the west side between 34th and 39th Streets (that's right -- 5 blocks long). This magnificent structure was attraction enough but I thought that with the powerboat industry closing out its finest year to date sparking great renewed interest in boating, the New York show could again become the important show that it once was.

The Jacob K. Javits Convention Center -- what a building! The entire east side of the structure for a length of five blocks is <u>all</u> <u>glass</u> -- a glazier's and window washer's delight. I'm not talking just doors and windows, but the whole facade and the walls and <u>roof</u> of the magnificent crystal palace lobby. This place could give Robert Schuller Crystal Cathedral in California a good run for its money. The mechanics of this structure are rather unique unless you are familiar with <u>Tinker</u> <u>toys</u>. Yes, the basis of this structure is Tinker toys! A simple round ball is bored in six or eight planes to accept rods. These balls form the connecting points for trusses and girders just like your old Tinker toy set! Inside the building, you are greeted by a maze of unhidden structure supporting all the glass. Unless you are a structure buff, you may not appreciate the naked unadorned trusses, columns, gussets, etc., but I certainly did. And where else could you stand among glittering fiberglass pleasure craft while looking out the face of the building at a full blown snow storm. Yes, on the opening day of the show, Friday, January 2nd, it was snowing.

You know, there is something special about looking at boats in a warm protected brightly lit environment when the weather outside is absolutely rotten. It makes one want to buy boats. Doesn't make sense, does it? Somehow, walking through the aisles of boats and knowing the weather was so bad outside made me want to buy a boat <u>right</u> <u>now</u>. It's contrast. At the Miami Boat Show, the weather is beautiful inside and outside. Beautiful boats are at the show, and surrounding the show at marinas and homes statewide. They are all around you. The boats inside are nothing special. In New York we are talking real contrast. Outside is the forbidden gray, dingy, cold, dirty, snowy, city and inside the glass palace are gleaming fiberglass, chrome and wood boats ready to take you to far off places away from the oppressive city. Ready to set you free! WHERE DO I SIGN!

From this writer's standpoint, the New York Boat Show of 1987 was an unqualified success. The main floor was packed with exhibits and, if the truth be known, there were exhibitors begging for more space. This means that next year the show will be even grander (there is another level available downstairs). The queen of the show was a Bertram 54 SF. Now I know that we have had 70'ers displayed ashore at Miami and 90'ers in Genoa, but I predict that in a few short years, New York will be fully competitive with these shows. Reasons? The magnificent convention center, the cold winter climate, the location in a major city of the world and the boom in boating in general.

Roaming around the isles of the boat show, these are some of the unusual things that my skewed mind noted compared to other shows:

1. More financial institutions with displays simply <u>begging</u> one to take their money to buy a boat. It seemed like every other display was a money lender ready to stuff bills in your pockets as you walked by. PLEASE... TAKE MY MONEY!

2. More displays for recreational rowing boats than I have seen at any other show. This is strange since you can only "recreational row" in the northeast for perhaps six or seven months of the year.

3. Boat salesmen were better dressed.

4. A jet drive outboard motor brought about, no doubt, by foolish liability claims against manufacturers of propeller drive systems.

5. A silly video trying to hype a speedboat. One of the big pitches was "strength and rigidity that lasts the life of the boat". What a foolish thing to say! When the strength and rigidity are gone and the bottom drops out, the life of the boat is <u>over</u> be it in 30 days or 30 years. Call it safe advertising (but I guess nobody will ever sue them over <u>that</u> statement).

6. The hot dogs are outstanding.

As a hot dog connoisseur and aficionado, I have sampled hot dogs around the world. The best are Nathan's Famous followed closely by Nedicks and Howard Johnsons (before they got greedy and went to an inferior jumbo). At German boat shows they serve a light color wurst of some kind without a roll that one eats like a celery stalk. One-quarter star. At Genoa, Italy, they don't have hot dogs at all. At Norwalk, hot dogs are soggy and limp (boiled?) served on stale buns. One-half star. At San Diego they serve <u>avocado</u> hot dogs! One-eighth star. At Annapolis they are nondescript. One-quarter star. At Miami they are large, pale, flavorless affairs, looking like inflated footballs. One-half star. But at New York, the hot dogs were spicy, firm and meaty with zesty bouquet, delicate aroma and excellent color. They were served up on a fresh bun with tangy mustard of the Gulden variety. Three and one-half stars! They're cooked on one of those funny grills with the rotating rollers. You are best advised to select one from the back of the rack for it is there that the well done dogs reside.

Roaming through the show, it was noted that the boats were decently displayed and there was a great enthusiasm amongst both showgoers and exhibitors. But there was one exhibit that simply blew me away. After chastising the boating industry for its bland, unimaginative crowded displays at the Fort Lauderdale Boat Show it was truly refreshing to see Storebro's display. Storebro builds quality cruisers in Sweden. Had they displayed their 34'er as other manufacturers were displaying their boats, it would have been just another nice boat. This year Storebro simply outdistanced the competition as far as display and showmanship goes. For the New York Boat Show, they displayed <u>half</u> of a 34'er. I don't mean the bottom half without the top. Bare hulls have been displayed before. That's nothing special. No, with considerable guts Storebro took a <u>saw</u> down the <u>centerline</u> of one of their beautiful, completed boat and displayed half of it. It was just like looking at an inboard profile drawing. All joinery, machinery and decor were in place. Towels were in their racks, dishes were in the galley just like there were half-people living aboard. You could clearly see stringers, frames, coring, joinerwork, glass work, etc., etc. A truly outstanding display and one, I am sure, to be copied in the future. The display does, however, raise some interesting questions. Was it brought about by a spiteful divorce settlement? Is this a new installment method of buying a boat? What the hell happened to the other half? When the show circuit is completed with the two halves be glued together and used as a whole boat again? Is Storebro in the process of developing a catamaran? Did the husband want a sportfisherman while the wife wanted a cruiser? In the meantime, while we are wondering about all this, Storebro must be complimented for the most innovative display seen anywhere in a good number of years.

When you leave the never-never land of the boat show, you are back out in the cold, harsh city fighting crosstown traffic to get home. In a sea of yellow cabs, you realize that New York cabbies have to be the worst in the world. Other cities have crazy cabbies (Rio, Genoa and Hong Kong come to mind) but they are skillful-crazy. They drive fast with bravura, brake hard and dart in and out but they do it well and, most of the time, you end up actually <u>admiring</u> the way these guys drive, even though, in the process, you have messed your pants! New York cabbies, on the other hand are either too stupid or too inconsiderate to realize what they are doing. They hog two lanes, cut you off, stop short for a fare, tailgate, run stop lights, lean on their horns, etc., etc. All this is accomplished with a "screw you, buddy" attitude unmatched anywhere in the world. Driving my Hertz-rented Volvo (in a rental car you do things you would not do in your own car) I thought I was more than a match for these yellow demons but I soon found there are no way to compete with their inconsiderateness, stupidity and recklessness.

The New York Boat Show? Look for it to become one of <u>the</u> shows of the season as it grows and gets more elaborate in its beautiful new home. The New York Boat Show started at the old Madison Square Garden at the turn of the century, moved to Grand Central Palace, then moved an armory in the Bronx (a boat show in the Bronx?) and then to the coliseum uptown. The early shows at the garden featured a huge water filled tank in which many of the boats were displayed <u>afloat</u>. That was showmanship par excellence! Now that the New York show had found a new, permanent home, we look for more of the same in the future. Pass the mustard. Hold the relish.

March 1987

About the Author

Tom Fexas was born in Queens, NY in 1941. He was a yacht designer extraordinaire with more than 1,000 boats to his design. His most famous design is the Midnight Lace - "While there are many 'classic cruisers' available on the market today, few have the heritage of the Midnight Lace, although the first Midnight Lace was completed in 1978, the Lace heritage goes back much further than that — back to the pre-World War II commuter boats and World War II PT boats creating a distinctive vessel that will never be mistaken for anything else.", in his own words.

He also had a sharp sense of humor, an observing eye for everyday life and wrote for several nautical magazines for more than 20 years.

Made in the USA
Monee, IL
08 April 2024